FULL

FINDING THE AUDACITY

OF

TO LOVE WHO YOU ARE

HERSELF

SARAH T. MOORE

FULL OF HERSELF

Finding the Audacity to Love Who You Are

MooreSoulSessions.com

Published by The Press Publishing | ThePressPublishing.com

Edited by Clare Fernández | ClareFernandez.com

Book Design by Transcendent Publishing | TranscendentPublishing.com

Front and back cover photos by Cheyenne Gil
About the Author photo by Amanda Wiggins Martin

ISBN: 979-8-9888988-0-1

Disclaimer: While some names have been changed, the stories in this book are personal anecdotes from the author's perspective. Care has been taken to give credit where credit is due when it comes to quotes and interactions with the ideas of others.

Printed in the United States of America.

"Everything we know is subject to revision, especially what we know about the truth."

— The Basic Text of Narcotics Anonymous

Contents

For women who want to stop fighting with themselves
and the world and who yearn to feel at peace
with who they are.

The stories in this book are ones that I want to tell. They are not in chronological order. Expect a blend of personal stories and coaching tools. I specifically chose this structure because it mirrors how I lead my live coaching events. Some moments are loud and energetic, other moments call for quiet reflection. I use pacing as a catalyst for reflection and growth. I'm also a lover of variety. I work best by having a few small tasks to keep me energized and engaged. This book reflects my preferences. Enjoy the journey.

Introduction

> "We have two lives. The life we live,
> and the unlived life within us."
> — Steven Pressfield, *The War of Art*

In my work as a life coach, I have heard the fears and desires of women across the globe, and every conversation boils down to one fear and one desire. The fear is about grappling with self-doubt, and the desire is to have more confidence.

Confidence is both personal and universal. That's why our stories matter. When we explore confidence for ourselves, we have the privilege of adding to the rich tapestry of experience and possibility that makes it more accessible for other women.

Many of my clients come to me trying to figure it out—a job, a relationship, a dream, whatever "It" Is. I help them unlearn how to "figure it out" and instead learn to let go, to become a little more vulnerable.

I want this for you, too.

You can become full of yourself if you have the courage to believe that every moment in life is a teachable moment. Even when you feel like you're flat on the floor, unable to move, sobbing your heart out ... There is *something* good leading you toward a better awareness of self.

In this book, I share intimate stories of my shortcomings and heartaches that are bursting with courage and wisdom. They're conduits for reflecting on the trajectory of your own life. For exploring the unlived life within you. For defining what full of herself means to *you*.

I believe the most effective life coaches are the ones modeling the work alongside their clients. As your life coach for the duration of this book, I will be your best supporter, especially in the tiniest of moments, because we all need to feel seen and heard in the everyday living of our lives. While I will always experience ups and downs, I have an abundance of tools and insights, and I know how to use them and share them with others.

The compliment I receive the most is, "Wow, Sarah, I love your energy." The way I like to say that is, "I'll have what she's having." You feel the sass of that other woman as you say those words. You know how magnetic she is. For me, that's my full-of-myself energy radiating out into the world and people reflecting back its power. Because oh baby is it powerful!

As Marianne Williamson says in her book, *A Return to Love*, "Our deepest fear is not that we are inadequate. Our deepest fear is that we are powerful beyond measure."[1]

As a woman who loves the journey of getting to know herself, even when it's hard, I have become very intentional about exploring the unlived life within me and sharing what I discover. Keeping hold of my desires and letting go of the outcomes is a life well-lived. A life of more ease, adventure, emotional maturity, and contribution—both when I err and when I succeed.

I hope this book helps you think about yourself and your behavior more holistically. In a world that doesn't want women to become full of themselves, I believe you have a responsibility to do so. Most people think of being full of themselves as something that's negative. It's arrogant. It's conceited. It's overconfident. My goal is to flip this idea on its head and have it be something that every woman desires to embody.

---

[1] Marianne Williamson, *A Return to Love: Reflections on the Principles of "A Course in Miracles"*, 1st ed. (New York: HarperCollins, 1992), 165.

To be full of yourself is your gift to yourself and the world and a pathway to liberation.

Let me remind you now that you are powerful beyond measure. *Full of Herself* is about normalizing and minimizing *your* self-doubt, inspiring you to find *your* confidence and power, to have the audacity to fall in love with the woman *you* are, and to share her with the world.

I'll see you on this brave and wild journey.

With love,

Sarah
x

I'm Not a Cheerleader

I've been on a journey to become a woman who cheers for other women. This has not been my natural state for most of my life.

In the past, I never liked it when other women would win. I wanted to win. I wanted to be the best. I wanted to be the center of attention. I wanted to be the only one doing exciting things. I wouldn't call myself malicious. I would call myself scared. It's amazing the havoc that fear can wreak.

If someone else shared something insightful, I was annoyed. If someone was thinner than me, I was annoyed. If someone did something outside the box, I was annoyed. It's fair to say that I was annoyed a lot. I wanted everything to be about me.

When I was 16, I went on an expedition to Costa Rica with my high school. We spent five weeks in community together: climbing Mount Chirripó (the highest mountain in Central America), building a playground, trekking through rainforests and along deserted beaches, speaking Spanish, and getting to know a largely undeveloped country back in 1999. I loved the whole experience.

When I came home, I was the girl who boasted about everything we'd done. I was sure that anyone who wasn't on the trip couldn't understand what a life-changing experience we'd had. The reality was that I didn't want them to understand. I wanted to feel different, separate, superior. Feeling "better than" kept my self-esteem whole. Boasting was my middle name.

Around this same time, someone told me that they were going scuba diving. Who they were or where I was, I can't quite recall, but I remember this moment like it was yesterday. I launched into a whole diatribe about how I learned to scuba dive at 11, how I was too young to even be certified at that age, and all the places in the world where I had dived. I wanted them to know how cool *I* was. This wasn't my moment, and I made it about me—in the name of feeling good about myself.

It wasn't intentional. It was the only way I knew how to feel important and find a momentary rush of joy before the uneasiness returned. Today, I think this has to do with the effects of alcoholism in my home growing up. When I was young, my parents constantly praised me, so wanting to be the best was part of how I showed up.

If anyone did anything I had done or gone anywhere I had been, I had to brag about it. What I know now is that I bragged because I wanted to feel just as special. I didn't want others to think they were better than me. And if someone was going somewhere I hadn't visited, I would feel annoyed (there's that word again). I would even find fault in the details of their vacation to prove that it wasn't "real" travel, which would mean I wasn't missing out on anything. *They're idiots. They don't know how to travel. They're staying in an all-inclusive resort. Pfff. That's not traveling. That's being a tourist, and it's tacky.*

I wouldn't have made this link at the time, but further reflection tells me that I was really saying, "By all means necessary, I will keep my self-esteem intact."

I've used the word annoyed several times. It was deeper than that. What I felt was jealousy, grief, insecurity, loneliness, and fear.

What's sad and funny to me now is that what they were doing had nothing to do with me. I think I am just now realizing the extent to which I allowed other people to dictate how I lived my life, instead of living my own.

It's only in writing this book that I have seen a radical transformation with regard to cheering other women on. I have started to feel elated for friends who are moving across the country, who are going on a big holiday, or who made a lot of money from a business deal. It has taken me by surprise. *I'm really cheering? Without any other thought except the cheer, most of the time. Wow. That's new and cool.*

I believe I have been moving in this direction of cheering for other women, little by little, for years. Cheering for others aligns with the woman I desire to be, and seeing my thoughts in writing has helped me expand this version of myself. I'm at a place in my beliefs where I know there is room for everyone to thrive and win. Being a cheerleader feels and sounds like maturity, and I'm into that because I want the perks of being an adult. When you win, I win. When you win, I get to see it's possible for me, too. Thank God that today I can know this truth in my bones.

Bullied

At the ages of 10, 14, 16, 17, 18, 20, and 21, respectively, I had a best friend who decided she no longer wanted to be my friend. Seven best friends gone. The pain of losing these friendships set my little heart adrift, and I started pretending and performing to cope. I would tell lies about how great my day was. I would boast to make myself feel better. I would exclude others to feel important. Being bossy gave me a sense of power. I did what I thought I needed to do to "fit in."

From the ages of four to 12, I attended an all-girls private school. When I was 11 and transitioned from primary school to secondary school, the trouble started. The class sizes in the school were very small. There were two classes of about 11 girls in each. Great student-to-teacher ratio, not so great when you're looking for somewhere to hide.

Three girls started bullying the rest of us. These girls were snarky and mean. I was a decent athlete, yet I was often picked last or second to last for every sports class. I felt embarrassed and sad every time someone got picked before me. Plus, my best friend now had a new best friend and, of course, they happened to be in my class.

At my private school, we had the equivalent of an "out of uniform" day, known as mufti day in England. We got to wear our own clothes rather than our posh navy blue uniforms. That year on mufti day, I wore these new, leather high-heeled boots that clickety-clacked very loudly down the long school hallway. The three bullies were behind me laughing, and I wanted to run out of those boots, yell at my mum for buying them, and never come back. Could they have been laughing at something else? That never occurred to me until now.

One time, they snickered at me in drama class when I stood up to perform. That was a class I loved, where I had great potential, and their stares made me feel timid and unsure. Another day, I took three or four paracetamols (Tylenol) so my stomach would hurt, and I'd be able to go home to avoid their taunting.

Yet another time, they accused me of abusing my pony—which was absolutely not true—and I told them they had done way worse to me. When they told the deputy headmistress what I had said, I was asked to apologize. I refused. It was the first time in my life I distinctly remember speaking up for what I thought was right. It was also the first time I realized, *Just because you're an adult, you don't know best.*

I did have one good friend, Rachel, who I loved. Rachel's mum didn't like me (I have no idea why), so we never went to each other's houses. We never walked out of the school gates together because Rachel didn't want to be seen with me in front of her mum. I'm realizing that we also never talked on the phone in the evenings as young girls typically do. I feel a real sadness about that now. The pretending was painful.

The bullying at that school was so bad that I transferred to a new school with hopes of leaving my despair behind. While I made plenty of new friends, I also lost several friends, too. One particular friendship with a girl named Fiona stands out. I couldn't believe that Fiona was my friend. We were 16, and she marched to the beat of her own drum. She worked a part-time job at a clothes store where we all shopped. She was *cool.* I would go to her house after school, which happened to be close to my mum's work, and hang out until it was time to head home. I loved this girl.

About a year into our friendship, she decided she no longer wanted to be my friend. *Here we go again.* We didn't have a conversation about it. One day we were friends and the next we weren't. I remember feeling left out and confused, lost and lonely. Fiona and I were part of a group of 10 girls. We would all party together at the weekends, celebrate birthdays, and get ready together before going out.

Well, after Fiona and I ceased to be a duo, I was somewhat in and somewhat out of the group. Looking back, I remember knowing that Fiona had made her decision. We were done. While it was hard to pretend that I was ok on the outside while feeling deeply hurt on the inside, I had a healthy respect for her boundaries.

It's clear to me now that I didn't understand Fiona's experience. I decided to reach out and ask her about it, even though we've had little contact for over 14 years. We have exchanged a couple of Facebook messages on various subjects as if nothing had happened—but that's it.

So when I started to write this book, I sent her a message. I took a couple of shaky breaths and asked her why she no longer wanted to be friends with me way back when, and then I proceeded to cry. As I was crying, I put my head in my hands and said with a smile, "Is this what writing a book is going to be like? Holy shit, this is only day one."

Fiona has not yet responded.

As I was the common denominator in all these situations, I have had to learn how to become a friend. Friendship makes me feel unsure to this day, and I continue to do my best to lean into it. I so admire people who have a big group of friends that they have had for years. That has not been my experience. My history, up until about age 30, is leaving people and places behind. At the age of 35, I left Philadelphia, where I lived for eight years. That was the first time in my life that I left a place and have remained friends with people.

Being bullied left a mark on my heart. It has been a big part of my story, and here's how I'm starting to transform the way I think about it.

During the process of writing this book, I connected with Tracy—one of my childhood bullies. The exchange that we had over Facebook Messenger was incredibly cathartic for me. We had a dialogue back and forth for months, and I'll be forever grateful that she was willing to engage in that conversation.

Tracy's memories of our school were pretty dismal. She described it as "stuffy, overly formal, small, and bitchy." She said that she didn't thrive there, and it became worse for her as the years went on. Tracy was kind enough to apologize over and over again for her part in my experiences.

Here's what got me the most. I shared with her that on my last day before transferring to my new school, when everyone signed my shirt, another of the bullies wrote, "You're a pig." Tracy said, "I don't remember ever thinking anything like that of you."

And there it was.

Another version of a story that undid mine in a split second. I thought they didn't like me and maybe, as Tracy shared with me, they were simply bored.

It was wondrous and baffling to hear that the story didn't exist in the same form on the other side. As I read her words, "I don't remember ever thinking anything like that of you," I cried. I let go. I wondered if I had made the whole thing up. Were there flaws in my story? Of course there were, and it doesn't make my experiences any less real.

What if the bullying wasn't about me? Was it my own lens that warped the experience into something else? Was it the perfect storm of my insecurity coupled with bitchy girls?

What if I wasn't bullied? What if I didn't know how to fit in and that was ok? What if my lack of self-worth got in the way of my ability to belong and pushed people away? What if they only reflected back to me what *I* thought about myself? What if it was never about them?

As all these questions swirled around in my head, I came to understand, in a new way, the power of our minds and our stories. A story that had been so well told by me that the pathway was practically a concrete road. And from childhood no less, before my brain had even fully developed. The interaction with Tracy gave me pause as I reevaluated life, my thinking, and my relationship with having been bullied. It's clear that a commitment to healing can reveal opportunities to transform deeply rooted and painful stories. That awareness feels empowering and disorienting.

Maybe, after 30 long years, I could forgive Tracy, the other bullies, and myself. Maybe I could move forward without that story interfering with the now.

What Do I Mean
When I Say God?

I will refer to God many times in this book. God is central to my life. Let me explain what God means to me so this isn't a stumbling block.

Common themes among my clients are perfection and control. They want to feel certainty. Do the following phrases sound familiar?

> *I need a five-year plan. Why don't I have one? Isn't this what successful people have?*

> *I don't think I'll bother saying anything. She's not going to change anyway.*

> *Why did I say that? I'm so stupid.*

> *What's the right answer?*

We want to know exactly where we're headed and how we're going to get there. We want to know that the hard conversations will turn out well. We berate ourselves when we fall short of our expectations, or the situation doesn't turn out as we hoped.

To be in control gives us a sense of certainty, or so we think. What my clients want more than being in control is to unlearn control. They don't know this when we start working together. What they really want is to experience flow. To stop wrestling with what isn't and allow what is. To unclench their fists and gently hold them open, ready to receive. They want to learn how to dance with the magic of life.

For me, that magic is God.

When I say God, I am referring to a Higher Power. Jesus, Buddha, something greater than us, nature, the universe, source, Shiva—whatever resonates with you. I don't believe God has any one form.

I believe the gateway to unlearning control—and in turn, developing a relationship with a Higher Power—comes through spirituality. I use the word spirituality because it's broad enough to encompass many approaches to embracing God and letting go.

I often ask my clients, "If I were to ask you about your spiritual life, how would you respond?" The first response is often that they don't identify as religious. The second is that they haven't thought much about their spiritual life at all or that they used to feel a spiritual connection and currently feel distanced from it. Most of the time, my clients report that this area feels uncharted. A little blank.

It's surprising—and at the same time unsurprising—to me that so many people confuse spirituality with religion. More than anything, it leaves me feeling a little sad. For some, they might be one and the same. For others, that might not be true.

Religion seems so specific, so black and white, so full of boundaries, so prescriptive, responsible for so much hurt. I also see religion as being a source of great comfort to many. Spirituality, on the other hand, feels soft, open, welcoming, inclusive. It's a source of comfort without restriction. I'll put it this way: I know that the odds of finding someone who has been harmed by religion are high. I can't think of a single person I have met who has been harmed by spirituality.

I don't talk to my clients about religion because I don't know religion. I instead talk to them about getting out of their own way. I believe that life is best lived if you're willing to admit that there's room for a little magic along the way. I know that it's unsustainable for me to drive (control) everything in my life. I need to learn how to not force outcomes, to be open to surprise, to sit back and allow space for life to happen, and for things and people and moments to come together.

Living life this way is what I call spirituality or being aligned with God. My clients want to experience living this kind of life even if they don't use these words to describe it. I translate their frustrations and open the door to spirituality. They get to decide how it might apply to their lives, which is the fun part, and, to date, I have been met with curiosity and openness on the subject.

Spirituality reminds me that it's not all about me and that my humanity has limits. I'm reminded to chill the fuck out. I am in constant need of this reminder. I want to release my grip on life and allow it to unfold with ease. I want to take time for reflection and connect with my inner self. I want to be able to answer with clarity: What do I really think, feel, fear, and desire? If I don't know the answers to these questions, I have work to do.

When I don't take the time for personal reflection, to sit and think quietly with myself, I don't consistently make decisions with integrity. Integrity means that your actions and values are in alignment. In my personal experience, centering spirituality in my life is the pathway to alignment.

There are so many ways to develop my spiritual life, to get closer to God. For me, it isn't a routine I check off in the morning. It's a constant series of actions that create alignment, delight, gratitude, discomfort, and awareness throughout my day.

I aspire to have every action in my day bring me closer to God. Working out and stretching, taking a cold shower, putting on a nice outfit, doing work that's meaningful, eating nourishing food, doing the hardest thing first, resting, loving my people well, growing, feeling uncomfortable, trying not to make a mountain out of a molehill, getting my nails done, sleeping, respecting my money, keeping a lovely home, keeping an open mind, forgiving myself and others, crying, punching a pillow.

All these acts, and so many more, attend to my well-being and bring me home to myself. They help me to stay full of myself. I get giddy thinking about how universal our lists are likely to be, how we all have similar wants and needs, how we are connected with each other and with God. That's what makes for good stories. The specifics of each of our stories are the adventure.

The Power of "And"

What we think and feel can be most honestly characterized by "and."

I'm grateful **and** sad.

I feel confident **and** needy.

I like you **and** I'm not sure.

I want the promotion **and** I'm wondering if I'm good enough.

I want to go **and** it feels like a hassle.

I can have different beliefs **and** respect you.

I can vote differently **and** enjoy dinner with you.

We often use "but" when what we really mean is "and."

When do you ever feel only one emotion or have only one thought? The answer for me is: rarely.

We're complex beings, and we're supposed to experience the full spectrum of emotions available to us.

"But" negates what came before it. "But" feels like resistance, like low energy, like I'm dragging my feet. *I don't want to do the washing, **but** I will. I don't want to work out **but** I guess I'll do it.*

"And" feels like energy, like momentum, like flow. *I don't want to do the washing, **and** I will. I don't want to work out, **and** you know what,*

I will. "And" creates agency. Agency is the feeling of having control over one's actions and their consequences.[2]

Let's take another example: *I want to tell her how I feel,* **but** *I don't want to disappoint her.* What I'm actually saying is that I don't want to tell her how I feel because the weight of disappointment is heavier than wanting to be honest. "But" is a way of undoing what I said, an avoidance of revealing my truth. "But" can indicate that I'm lying to myself. When I replace "but" with "and," both options become true. *I want to tell her how I feel,* **and** *I don't want to disappoint her.*

"And" is more representative of life, of our emotional range. Life isn't either/or, black/white. It's often a mixture of the two. We can have the desire to be honest *and* be afraid of the outcome. That reveals some vulnerability, some nuance.

When I feel stressed, I have a tendency to resort to extreme, dramatic thinking. In these moments, "and" is a lovely tool to remind me that more than one thing can be true at a time, opening a door to self-compassion.

We are still going to use the word "but." I know I do. It's appropriate at times. A good "but" can feel satisfying. There are other moments where I say "but" when "and" is the better option. For me, "and" represents the greater whole of who I am rather than backing myself into a corner and pitting my beliefs—which are supposed to live alongside one another—against each other.

"And" for greater humanity toward ourselves. "And" for honesty.

---

[2] James W. Moore, "What Is the Sense of Agency and Why Does It Matter?" Frontiers in Psychology, U.S. National Library of Medicine, August 29, 2016, https://www.ncbi.nlm.nih.gov/pmc/articles/PMC5002400/.

Once you start replacing "but" with "and," you'll notice how often you contradict your feelings. To practice this skill, dive into the exclusive workbook I've created for you at:

mooresoulsessions.com/workbook

Sexual Assault

When I was a student at The University of Sheffield in England, I lived with a group of five friends. We all studied languages and had spent our third year abroad living in various parts of the world. One of my flatmates and I lived in Argentina for part of that year, and we were all excited to return to Sheffield to complete our studies.

Only a couple of weeks upon returning, I was sexually assaulted. It was a shock to have this happen in Sheffield, a city I knew well, after having traveled pretty extensively throughout South America.

I didn't know the guy; he was serving our table at a friend's birthday. It was a big group and we were all having loads of fun. I later woke up in the restaurant bathroom. I've no idea how I got there. When I emerged, the restaurant was empty and my friends were gone. I walked outside, and our waiter was parked on the street. He offered to drive me home.

When we pulled up to my flat, he tried to force himself on me in the car. As I'm writing this, I'm crying because I don't remember the details, and I feel ashamed about that fact, which is an interesting response. When I pushed him away, he ejaculated on me. I was able to frantically open the car door and get out. Thankfully he didn't rape me.

As I walked into our flat, tears running down my cheeks, one of my friends laughed at me as I pointed out the ejaculation on my clothing. I remember thinking, *If she's laughing, maybe what happened isn't that serious.* The next morning, another flatmate encouraged me to go to the police. I did, and when they asked how much I had to drink, I told them less than was true. I instinctively felt that I had to lie to be taken seriously.

When I returned from the police station, I told my remaining flatmates what had happened, and they showed little to no support. A couple of them tried to blame the situation on the fact that I had been drinking. I felt abandoned by my friends' response. It felt like more proof that I couldn't count on people, that I didn't belong. Yet another moment of feeling let down by people that I cared about. It felt like my whole life up to this point was a series of friends pushing me away.

What I haven't yet talked about is how *I* pushed my friends away and the part I played in these broken relationships. I wore my friend's coat several times without asking. I ate food out of our communal fridge that wasn't mine because I thought I could. I drank a lot to fit in. More importantly, I didn't know how to be intimate with people or myself, so I know I was challenging to be friends with.

Little things added up over time that caused people to see the parts of me that were not quite so charming and a little more broken. In many ways, I was a lost young woman, and I can see how my friends were fed up with me and my antics. I'm not excusing their response, and I do understand their lack of support. (See how I chose "and" instead of "but" there?)

It's a baffling thing to want to belong so badly. And yet, in trying to do so, I achieved the exact opposite.

A Desire to Belong

When I was younger, I desperately wanted to fit in and be liked because I have often felt like I didn't fit in and wasn't liked. Sometimes, I still feel that way, and I catch myself when I'm trying too hard. In my 20s, I didn't know what "fitting in" even meant. I just knew I wanted to feel different. I didn't want to feel unhappy, desperate, exasperated, and unsettled in myself. I didn't know that I was creating my own problems, that they didn't exist outside of me. I thought life was happening, that it creates itself, and, quite frankly, that it wasn't all it was cracked up to be.

When I was 25, I started working at a lingerie company. After 18 months, I was promoted to manager of a new store, and we had a week-long training session for new hires. The assistant manager hired to run the store with me had significantly more bra-fitting experience, and the company-wide trainer, Dawn, kept calling on her for insights during the training.

I felt insecure about that because I wanted to establish my authority as the manager. My choice of words here is not lost on me. I could be wrong, but I have a memory from that training of Dawn calling on me at the precise moment I wasn't listening, and, of course, I didn't know the answer. Something inside of me felt like it wasn't a coincidence. I also know it was my responsibility to listen.

One day, I sat with Dawn to eat. She shared that she loved college football and that it was a big event in her house. With my insecurity and resentment simmering, I said something to the effect of … wait for it … "I try to get away from college football as fast as I can." I'm dying slightly inside as I write this. Why would I say that?

Let me share the logic I operated with at the time.

Back then, I viewed college football as beneath me, a bit lowly, something that everyone watched. In my mind, what's more common in America than American football? It's such an obvious choice. So, dissociating myself from it felt, to me, more interesting, more elite. There was also a part of me that wanted to get back at Dawn for calling on me when she knew I wasn't listening. *Screw you and your football.*[3] I know, you guys. This was not a catch-a-fly-with-honey recipe.

What I wanted more than anything in the world was connection—to feel seen and heard and loved for exactly who I am and to make others feel the same in return. The mere thought of that intimate connection, however, left me feeling terrified because I thought others wouldn't like me if I showed them exactly who I am. So I unconsciously chose the strategies of being "different" and "better than" to push people away so I would feel safe, albeit lonely.

I didn't know that a strategy that works well for developing relationships with people is *to be interested in them.* I cared more about being the best and making it all about me. In my desperate effort to show Dawn how great I was and to will it true for myself (while feeling out of sorts on the inside, by the way), I pushed her away. I did exactly the opposite of what I wanted. It's easy to do this and not even realize it ... unless we work on our self-awareness consistently. I have learned that trying to show people how great I am is a miserable pursuit; so is trying to fit in.

Fitting in is about abandoning yourself—dressing how you think you should, saying what you think you should say, exaggerating or

---

[3] The funny thing here is that I now love college football! I follow my and Preston's alma mater, the Texas A&M Aggies, whether he's watching with me or not. Even my mum loves watching them. This is a great example of having no clue who I will one day become.

minimizing to assimilate. "Belonging, on the other hand, doesn't require us to change who we are; it requires us to be who we are."[4] I didn't want to fit in after all. What I desperately wanted was to belong. It would be a while before I understood the difference between fitting in and belonging. I'm still learning every day how to belong in a group and, above all else, how to belong to myself.

---

[4] Sandra Restreppo, dir. *Brené Brown: The Call to Courage*, Netflix, 2019, https://www.netflix.com/title/81010166.

Morning Routine

By nature, I am a fluid person. I don't like to do the same thing every day, at the same time. I love variety and choice and space to think and be. I also thrive on a good amount of structure to keep me focused and purposeful. And I like to call the shots on how the structure is structured.

Many of my clients feel wary of a morning routine because they, too, don't want to feel hemmed in by doing the same things every day. I'm going to tell you what I tell them: put together an arsenal of tools to pull from so that during your morning time you can choose what best satisfies your needs for that day.

Make a list of three to five things you can do to quiet your nervous system and raise your emotional state. This way, you have choices without feeling overwhelmed. From there, you can start to identify what's working and what isn't, what raises your vibration, and what you enjoy. Fine-tuning this process will take time, so be patient.

My core tools are journaling, reading my 12-step literature, and meditation. I often work out first thing in the morning as well; that way it's done, and I don't talk myself out of it. I like the feeling of finishing my workout before I've fully woken up and starting my day off with something hard. During my workout there is always a moment, and usually several, when I think, *If I can finish this workout, I can do anything that comes my way today.* My workout primes me for hard things which helps me to feel accomplished and hopeful.

My ideal amount of time for myself in the morning is three hours. It gives me time to think, be, evolve, reflect, and practice some of my tools. During this time, I find myself getting exceptionally creative and clear on what I want. I don't get nearly as much out of my life if I land full speed into my day.

Sometimes I spend two hours going through a routine and then running some errands. Sometimes I want to get out of the house because I work from home. I'll go to Starbucks and get the only drink I buy from there—a tall decaf soy latte—which is one way to my heart. Sometimes I do a great breathwork session, make some bone broth, and get to work on coaching or our real estate business. Some days I have a cold shower, and I hit the ground running. Some days I may only get an hour to myself in the morning due to school runs and work demands.

No matter how much time you have, whether it's 10 minutes or two hours, find some tools that work for you to start your day off right. If you're looking for some inspiration, here's my arsenal:

- Reading (for pleasure and work)

- Breathwork

- Meditation

- Listening to an inspiring talk

- Journaling

- Singing

- Saying nice things to myself

- Listening to music and dancing

- Taking a cold shower

- Stretching

- Foam rolling

- Going for a walk

- Working out

- Calling my 12-step sponsor

- Doing coaching homework from my coach

- Working on my 12 steps

- Reading 12-step literature

- Reaching out to people to tell them I'm thinking about them

- Sipping on homemade bone broth

My list of tools is long because I've had a morning routine for over a decade and have acquired many practices along the way. As such, I feel comfortable having a plethora of activities to choose from. If you're getting started or you're feeling unsure of how this routine could support you, my best advice is to start small, and most importantly, start.

I love the freedom to pay attention to what I need in the moment and pull out my tools accordingly. I also love the discipline and structure I have created to consistently do my work. I'm always in the flow of doing my work. It's who I am. Who I'm becoming as a result of this intentional time is the biggest gift of all. I wish the same for you.

What Do I Think?

When I was going through a treatment program for depression and suicidal thinking, my therapist told me that the four most devastating words in the English language are, *What will they think?*

The question hit me like a ton of bricks. As I started to piece together my story and see it from a new vantage point, I realized that I had been living my life feeling very worried about what other people thought of me. It surprised me because I didn't think I was living that way.

I worried about people finding out how much money I make. I worried about how hard my husband Preston thought I was working. I worried if I looked thin enough to my parents who are slim and active. I worried that people thought I was stuck up. I worried that I shared too much. The worries were—and still can be—endless. When the question, *What will they think?* became so devastating, the immediate antidote for me was, *What do I think?*

This question has become my most important tool that emerged from a hard, hard period. It is a guiding light in my life, so much so that I had it tattooed on my wrist two years after completing the treatment program. It's my first and only tattoo. Getting that tattoo felt like a big moment. A moment when I had traveled far enough from that hard experience for it to settle in my bones, when I became willing to change my body forever, and when I knew what it meant to practice, day in and day out, asking myself, *What do I think?*

As I applied the question in every corner of my life, it gave me more of a voice and showed me where I was being codependent and living out other peoples' stories. As a coach and as a woman, I want to make a stand for the question, *What do I think?*

I know from all my years of coaching experience that so many women are struggling to find their voices. Why? Because they're too focused on and worried about the opinions of others.

Here are some examples of *What do I think?* in action.

Scenario 1—Internal Dialogue:

I feel like people are looking at me a lot in this outfit.

What do I think?

I think I feel hot. Great, then I'll own it.

Or …

I don't like the fit of this skirt. I don't feel great in it. Ok, I'll donate it or sell it because I want to feel good in my clothes.

Scenario 2—Client Conversation:

Client: I feel like my boss thinks I'm high maintenance.

Me: What evidence do you have to support that feeling?

Client: Last week, he told me that he doesn't need to check all my work.

Me: How often do you ask him to check your work?

Client: Often. I'm still new in the role, and it gives me confidence.

Me: Do you believe you're high maintenance?

Client: A little, perhaps.

Me: It also sounds like you might be asking for what you need. Does that make you high maintenance?

Client: I don't know, does it?

Me: What do you think?

Client: I guess not.

Me: It sounds like you're asking for what you need and that's helping you to progress further in your work. Perhaps you might take a moment and assess whether the amount of support you have been asking for is still what you need to feel confident.

Client: I believe it is, although I probably want to check in with myself every time before I ask.

Me: You got it. Excellent insight. You can ask for what you want no matter what someone else thinks. You might feel uncomfortable, and that's ok. Also, be aware of moments where you're over-relying on your boss's approval, when in fact you could give that to yourself. What moments can you think of when you have asked for his input this week and didn't need to?

Bonus follow-up question: How can that insight inform your ability to approve of yourself moving forward?

Scenario 3—Internal Dialogue:

I bet she thinks my house is messy.

Do I think my house is messy? Yes, I do.

Do I care? Yes. And, it's the best I've got today.

Scenario 4—Client Conversation:

Client: I told my boss that I was feeling upset about the meeting. Do you think I shared too much?

Me: What do you think? *(I'm asking my client to assess her own feelings first before reaching for someone else's input.)*

Client: I'm not sure.

Me: What are you not sure about?

Client: I think it's important I share how things affect me, and I don't want to seem too needy.

Me: Now that you're thinking about the interaction with a little distance, do you think you were needy? *(What her boss thinks matters less than what my client thinks about herself.)*

Client: Yes, I do. I want to talk about my feelings in a more empowered way.

Me: Great. Let's talk about how to do that …

Whatever your decision, in any scenario, it only matters what you think, not what others think. Resist the temptation to apologize because, most likely, you don't need to. The desire to do so is great because you want to manage what the other person thinks of you.

I did this just the other day (see Scenario 3). A friend of Austin's (my son) came to our house for the first time. When his mum came to the front door, I started telling her about the renovations we were doing in the living room. I didn't say I'm sorry, and I did explain myself. I wanted her to know that I usually keep a clean home. Why does it matter what she thinks? I care … and I don't care. Holding the tension of these opposing feelings is where transformation can begin. Me being comfortable *enough* in my skin is the goal, not trying to please someone else.

What do I think? brings me home to myself and keeps the focus on me. I can only control myself. There are two types of business: my business and none of my business.

I've created a signature 4-step process for practicing my favorite tool, along with even more of a personal peek into what I worry about. I'm excited to share this tool with you. Download it here:

mooresoulsessions.com/workbook

Self-Awareness

Learning how to have a sense of ease with myself and others and finding my place in the world is my soul's work. I call this self-awareness, and it's at the center of my world.

What do I mean when I say self-awareness? It's the process of getting to know oneself intimately.

My work as a coach is to share what I'm learning.

Knowing myself and my motivations is life-changing because I get to actively create my life. Most people spend their whole lives reacting to life without ever understanding why they feel frustrated. To boot, most of us don't even have the basic language and knowledge to know we're reacting. We think it's "just the way I am," or it's "my personality."

I'm doing my best to equip myself with the tools to keep growing. As humans, we are constantly evolving, which means we need to put in the work to know who we are. It's a bit like traveling; there is always a new person to meet, a delay to encounter, a lost bag to mourn, a new perspective to gain, a new mountain range to admire. Change is the constant we can count on.

What is the work of self-awareness? For me, wanting to grow comes naturally because I am very growth-oriented. I'm always eager to see the lesson and opportunities in everything. Plus, I am very sure that I was born to be a coach, so my desire and ability to make connections in human behavior are well attuned. More practically speaking, it's taking the time to sit and be quiet with myself, to reflect on what's working and what isn't, and course correct where I can.

I find that most people, including me, can ignore problems in the hopes that they will go away. We make it sound fancy and say that we struggle with procrastination. The greater truth is that we haven't developed the skill of reflection. Being self-aware means I'm able to listen. Listen to myself, listen to my body and thoughts, listen to God, listen to my intuition, listen to the whispers. From there, I can adjust my behavior if necessary. As a result, I can find my way through this life with more intention, purpose, and peace.

I believe that we are all here to become a version of ourselves that makes us proud. We have a responsibility to understand what drives us and excites us, and to shape our lives around those things so that we can make a unique contribution to this beautiful world. I think people struggle when they think they're supposed to find the one thing they were meant to do. It's great if you know what that thing is. If you *don't* know what it is and you're hyper-focused on trying to find it, you will miss the beautiful life you're living right now.

This narrowly focused approach is a recipe for frustration. Instead, pay attention to what moves you in the moment and keep evolving toward that. Share openly what you learn and who you become in that process. We're not born to be passive. We're born to contribute.

I'm clear that, among other things, I was born to learn how to express myself fully and to be a voice and example for other women to do the same. Plus, I need to be in a state where I can access my tools. My self-awareness practices create that ideal state.

Just as important as knowing who I am and how to live my life—not someone else's—I need to know when not to listen to myself. My thoughts and feelings are not always my friends and are definitely not always facts. Rather, they are moving targets that can create new blind spots.

This is why it's critical to my self-awareness that I have a professional coach, mentor, therapist, counselor, and/or support group in my corner. I don't know what I don't know, and I can't see what I can't see. It's awesome to have a good friend, mum, or sister to talk to—and it does not cut the mustard if they are your only outlets. They are too close to you and in the mud with you to see clearly.

I have had many great people in my corner over the years. Right now, I have a breathwork and life coach who I work with once a month. I have an Al-Anon sponsor—a mentor with more experience in the program than me—who I talk to several times a week. I have friends in Al-Anon, whose programs I respect and whom I call for help regularly. I have an Owaken breathwork subscription that I use to regulate my mind and nervous system.

I also have some great friends who are incredibly talented, many of whom are coaches, who enhance my life. Sometimes they tell me what I need to hear, which can be incredibly comforting. They also set me straight regularly. I will always have a professional and a free support group in my corner. As someone who thrives on getting to know myself, the stakes are too high not to.

Embracing "I Don't Know"

"**I** don't know" is one of the most underrated phrases in the workplace and in leadership.

Every single person I have coached—no matter their age, race, title, or tenure—struggles to tell the truth in their workplace. From feeling afraid that their idea sounds stupid to being actively discriminated against. From worrying about how they'll sound to working in a team that undervalues trust and engagement. If you think about it, it's absurd. Good people with lots of potential, talent, and creative thought are lacking the conditions to thrive.

They're also lacking the tools to create a prosperous environment for themselves when the conditions don't allow for it. That's why doing our work is paramount. We have to become people who can tell the truth and hear the truth. And sometimes that truth is saying, "I don't know."

Imagine this workplace scenario. The CFO asks Jennie in accounting a question, and she says "I don't know." Not because Jennie is negligent or lazy or unprepared but because this question hasn't come across her radar yet. Not because Jennie "missed" something—which is often language for tolerance, not acceptance—but because she is juggling 362 competing demands. She is able to say, "I don't know" because the CFO and the culture at her work genuinely allow her to not know.

In our current work culture, knowing the answers and having them ready at a moment's notice is prized. But we don't always know the answers, and pretending we do doesn't serve us. The heaviness of pretending is like body armor. It's a weight lifted when we choose to remove that armor and become more full of ourselves by being honest about what we don't know.

What if someone on your team said, "I don't know," and your inner reaction was, "Cool." What if you didn't slightly gasp on the inside, your heart beating faster upon hearing "I don't know"? Would that be an indication that your team is actually healthy? That it allows for vulnerability? What if Jennie followed, "I don't know," with, "Tell me more, Jim. Maybe I can answer that question right now with a little more information. If not, I'll circle back." What if Jennie had more questions than answers? What if Jim genuinely asked for input from the room, not to shame Jennie, but to leverage insights and create momentum?

Doesn't that scenario sound wonderful?

To the leaders reading this: In a world where employees are craving vulnerability in action, please model what it looks like not to have all the answers. It's impossible that anyone would. If they do claim to, I would question their integrity. When you don't know, say, "I don't know." And, when you do know, say what you do know. That level of transparency is what we crave and need in all areas of our lives. It's that simple.

The amount of politicking, pretending, and performing that happens in organizations blows my mind. I am so clear that working for myself works well for me. I have a low tolerance for smoke and mirrors, games and shame, and cultures that create environments where people are too damn scared to tell the truth.

We need to model—for younger folks coming up through the ranks especially—the value of not knowing so they can take some pressure off of their already burdened shoulders. They constantly feel like they have to be right or have the right plan to be of value. We can do better. It can start with, "I don't know."

Storytelling

Nothing gives me more joy than hearing someone's story. That's what I get paid to do, and I also do it for fun and for free. My main hobby is human behavior—learning about people, what makes them tick, and what inspires them—coupled with good ol' girly talk: sex, fashion, nails, design, travel, TV, and life. My form of digging deep isn't politics, it's you.

To get into the details of you is an absolute joy for me. I know that what I'm hearing changes the course of a conversation, a day, a career, a relationship, a life, a legacy, and generations of families. Every time I hear something true and real about someone's life, I get to internalize that information, applying to my life what works for me and what doesn't. I get to learn and grow.

Tell me something real about you, and that, for me, is a day well-lived because I experienced a real moment of connection in receiving the truth, and so did you, in getting to tell it.

I find people's lives to be a pursuit of creativity. How one person overcame adversity and how another followed her dream. The intricacies of how one person trusted the moment and how another decided to parent differently. Why did one person make this decision and one person make that decision?

Generally speaking, people fascinate me and give me hope. People inspire my next decision. We have no idea how we impact people, and I love that anomaly. As I once heard Lin-Manuel Miranda say, "Every time you make something, you're throwing rocks in a pond. You have no idea of the ripples that are going to come back to you."[5]

---

[5] R.J. Cutler, filmmaker. *Dear...* Season 1, Episode 2, "Lin-Manuel Miranda." Aired June 4, 2020. Cutler Productions, 2020, documentary.

Judgment

The modus operandi and secret weapon in my family has always been judgment. Secret because we wouldn't tell you what we were really thinking. I have since learned that we can communicate a lot in our silence.

In alcoholic homes, there tends to be a collective struggle with issues of self-esteem. When we have low self-worth, it's human nature to judge other people as a way to avoid our own pain. I believe that pattern has been passed down through several generations on both sides of my family.

While my family has softened over the years, here are some of the things we have judged. The actual list is much longer.

- People who wear cheap, plastic shoes (the headmaster at one of my schools growing up)

- People who wash their cars at the weekend

- People who go on cruises

- People who were going on holiday with their caravan (a pull-behind camper) while we were driving to Heathrow Airport to fly out to some exotic destination

- People who vote for Labour (political party in England)

- People who go to the local school rather than putting their kids in the best school they can

- People who eat ketchup

- Americans who go on holiday, to Europe especially, for *only* 7-10 days

- People with bad table manners (e.g. eating with their mouth open, not using a knife and fork properly)

- People who study degrees ending in "ology"

- People who own trucks and drive them like cars

- Expats who all live together and aren't really experiencing the culture

- Brits who go on package holidays (where everything is included) to Spain

- People with tattoos (so common—also, now, me)

- People who are fat and "big blobs" or who "have an arse like the back end of a bus"

So many people to judge. So many people to feel superior to. So many people to not let in. So much loneliness. So many unconscious behaviors. I have often judged other people very harshly for simply living their lives in a way that makes sense to them. Judging someone allows me to keep them at arm's length and forgo intimacy.

I am learning how to be a person who accepts people as they are. I am learning how to champion the decisions of others and to offer grace. I am learning how not to judge.

When I see you and hear you for who you are—a core attribute as a coach—I gain understanding, and through understanding comes love. Maybe I was drawn to coaching because it represented the opposite of judgment. I craved a safe space to be seen for exactly who I am. Today, these spaces heal me back to wholeness. Is it any wonder I now create safe spaces for others?

The last thing I want to feel is judged, so I do my best to repay the desire. When I judge someone, it now feels icky, and I move away from it as quickly as I can see and feel it. My judgment is as simple and as challenging as a reflection of a lack of love toward myself. Like with everything in life, it's about me, not the other person. Working on not judging myself will forever be a goal in this lifetime.

I am learning how to feel safe with people. And that starts with me learning how to feel safe with myself. The more I evolve as a person by continuing to do my work and the closer I get to people through their stories, the more impossible it becomes for me to lead with judgment.

Go Easy

Go easy on yourself, Sarah.

Take it easy.

Don't make it so hard.

Unclench your fists.

Ebb and flow.

Nice and easy.

And, relax.

And, breathe.

I could hear these words every day, and it would still feel like the first time. I'm more like a bull than a gazelle—I go barreling into everything with full force. My primal instincts tell me to *buckle down and make it happen.* Left to my own devices, I grunt and sigh more than I'm silent and breathing deeply. I force and push. I want to run away more than I want to stay. I overtalk and overthink. I'm learning to feel safe in this life, this body.

Many of these behaviors have served me well and contributed to my success. And I'm seeing how much of my life I don't enjoy because I'm rushing and living outside of the moment. Yesterday, I was worrying about a conference I'm speaking at on November 3. Today is September 14. Feeling this way is normal and also unreasonable to me. I'm learning how to live in the now and let today, September 14, be a great day.

I don't have to figure out all the things. The list doesn't have to be finished. Getting bogged down in the details of the list doesn't serve us either. If you have a long, running list that you consistently cross off and add to, ask yourself, "Does this list calm me or create more chaos?" When my clients pause long enough to get honest, they most often share two sentiments at once: "I love lists but they create more chaos." I encourage them to change this "but" to "and." Both things are true.

If that's true for you, too, scrap the long list. It's not so much the list itself as the way you're using it. A long list constantly reinforces that your work is never done, which creates feelings of overwhelm.

Try this instead.

Every morning, write down (this could also be a part of a journal entry) three or four things that you want to accomplish that day. You can also do this the evening before. Then, do them. I find three or four to be a manageable amount. These are the core things in your work and life that need attending to and that give you a sense of forward movement. That way, you're living in the present and going about tasks based on how you're feeling.

I want to be careful here. I'm not saying that you do tasks only when you feel like doing them. That isn't a recipe for success. I am saying that some days we have lots of energy and can get a lot more done, so you might do harder tasks that day, and/or do six instead of three. On other days, you might have the bandwidth to drop into a more important phone call and really hear the other person, so you choose that task.

A day-by-day approach, while still having short- and long-term goals, helps me to meet myself where I am and not get ahead of myself. It's also a great way to prioritize. I used to often write down ideas that weren't meant for now, and they would linger, staring back at me, teasing me for months.

The truth is I had no business adding them to the list. Can you honestly look at your long list and say that everything needs to be done? Or do you have superfluous items in the name of not holding them in your head that keep you scrabbling like a hamster on a wheel?

Instead, I started a creative list of business ideas on my phone that could serve as inspiration, something to revisit from time to time—*separate from a to-do list*. When I stopped making long lists, I couldn't believe how much extra work I had made for myself. And how those lists made me feel like crap and I didn't even realize it!

When I attend to my needs day by day, I allow room for the magic of life to unfold, which means accepting change. I change. Life changes. The needs and desires of my loved ones change. This means that shit that would have been on the list—that I very well might have wasted time doing—no longer serves a purpose. I evolved past it and because I'm unlearning the habit of finding my worth through how much I do, I don't waste my time and get ahead of myself. I live in today.

I often map out important things for the week and schedule them on my calendar. I love scheduling things on my calendar. *Call Mary. Follow up with the dentist. Pay Citi card. Write proposal.* While I choose a free time slot in my day to schedule it, I don't complete the task at that scheduled time. It's more of a reminder that *at some point today* this needs to get done. I enjoy the freedom to choose how to fit my tasks into my day. Scheduling in this way keeps all my commitments in one place.

I also have recurring meetings with myself on the calendar, such as a meeting twice a month on Friday mornings to review our finances and a real estate meeting every Sunday to review our Airbnb business. These important to-do's become a part of my routine rather than something I have to remember and schedule, which takes the pressure off my shoulders and creates clarity and ease.

People often confuse "urgent" and "important." Society has trained us to feel like every little thing is urgent, leaving very little room for ease in life. I don't have to do all the things to find ease. I don't *want* to do all the things to find ease. Most things are not as urgent as I think they are when I give myself some breathing room to consider my priorities. Urgency often equates to being busy. I'm not interested in being busy for the sake of being busy. I try to do the important things—what's meaningful to me and for me—*first* because they move the needle the most. That makes me feel really proud. And with that comes a sense of ease.

Go easy on yourself, Sarah.

Take it easy.

Don't make it so hard.

Unclench your fists.

Ebb and flow.

Nice and easy.

And, relax.

And, breathe.

What's in a Name?

When I was four, I started kindergarten. There were about 15 girls in my class. There were four Sarahs and, to boot, all named Sarah Louise. I was one of them. As a result, I was often referred to as Sarah T (my maiden name is Tonner). Practically, of course, it made sense for the teachers to use our surnames. There were times when I hated the T. It felt like a stain, an embarrassment.

I can't quite put my finger on why I hated it. I wonder if, at such a young age, I already felt adrift from myself, wanting to run from who I was. Did I feel as though I was in the wrong identity? Did I have an awareness that something was off in our family, namely alcoholism, even though I didn't know that at the time? I don't know, and I don't need to know. For some reason, the sound of my surname out of someone else's mouth made my stomach turn. I felt as though I didn't belong to myself. The T felt impersonal. I desperately wanted to be Sarah. Why wasn't Sarah enough?

Sometimes I wonder if the other Sarahs felt the same way. The world tells me I'm more than my name, yet a name is so personal, so familiar. Having a surname that made me feel uncomfortable is, to me, an interesting detail in a story about identity and getting comfortable with oneself.

While Tonner wasn't my favorite word as a young person, I became more comfortable with it as I matured. I never specifically worked through the frustration with my name. It seemed to take care of itself. It was interesting then to arrive at a place where, when I got married, I felt hesitant to give up Tonner. How curious that in a moment when I had the opportunity to let go of something that felt unsettling to me, I didn't.

It was almost as if I knew that I can't be Sarah without the T, without the Tonner. That the Tonner will always be a part of who I am. That I needed to integrate it if I am to feel whole with myself. Today, the T belongs to me. My legal name is Sarah Tonner Moore, and I still sign my name as S.T. Moore. Tonner is a big part of who I am that I accept and love. There is redemption in this work as I come home to myself and make sense of who I am.

Sarah was always enough. She just didn't know it.

Jennie and Charlie

My parents met in the Galápagos Islands in the late seventies. At the time, my dad was the Chief Engineer on a luxury passenger ship—of which he had overseen the building—in Bilbao, Spain. He sailed it from Spain to the Galápagos Islands where it was to be a permanent fixture hosting tourists and researchers.

My mum worked as a secretary for a travel agency in London that specialized in taking tours through the Galápagos Islands and the Amazon Rainforest. She was once asked to fill in for a tour guide who was on maternity leave. Mum enjoyed the work and was good at it, so she became a regular guide. The tours included visiting Galápagos and joining the passenger ship that Dad was on.

Mum and Dad connected several times and finally, on one of those tours, my mum decided to join my dad on a banana boat that he was sailing to Miami, Florida. Not long after arriving in Miami, my dad found another job four hours away in Tampa overseeing repairs to another ship that was in drydock. This decision to literally jump ship may seem crazy to many. To me, it's normal. To live life and seize the moment, as my parents always have, is the example I know like the back of my hand.

My mum left behind her life in London. Once in Tampa, they decided it was a nice place to live and bought a house. They lived on Davis Island, a small island connected to downtown, for seven years. Their real estate agent, a lady named Barbara whom they had never met before, lent my parents the money for the down payment while my dad waited for his next check to arrive. Talk about a lesson in generosity and kindness.

I can't say I would lend a stranger thousands of dollars, but then again, I want to be moved by Barbara's example and allow it to seep into my lived experience. I'm deciding, right now, that while this decision defied logic, it's absolutely the kind of moment I want to share with a stranger one day. Logic isn't close to the top of my preferred states of being anyway. I want to pass along what was so freely given to my parents: a new start, trust, hope, and connection through the transaction of money.

Barbara and her husband Chuck became good family friends and went on to become my godparents when I was born three years later. My parents paid $60,000 for a lovely house on that island where today you can't buy dirt for less than $1 million. *If only they could have held onto that house,* I have thought. *What a real estate story that would be.*

My parents have shared with me that they felt like two broken souls coming together to heal. They both left children and marriages behind to come together and form this new life. My home was an alcoholic home, although I didn't know that until my early twenties. There was turbulence because of the drinking and the learned behaviors that alcoholic families adopt. My parents also did a wonderful job raising me, giving me access to opportunities galore. There was a lot of love and fun and adventure.

As parents go, mine are awesome.

One of the things I heard most growing up was the phrase, *Go for it.* Going for it signified a desire and a belief that anything was possible. Want to win that competition? Go for it. Want to start a restaurant? Go for it (like my mum did). Want to go on a skiing holiday together? Let's go for it. Want to be the first female president of the United States? Go for it. Want to buy the nice dress? Go for it. You only live once.

Going for it is in my blood. It's a big part of what makes me tick. It brings me to life. It energizes me. It gets my heart pumping. It makes my eyes get wide like a kid seeing a big ice cream cone.

I'm forever grateful that my parents modeled adventure. They taught me that nothing is too big to want or dream and to take action with faith. I love that about them and me.

Tiniest of Moments

Most people revere and reminisce over the big moments. Moments like getting married, a promotion, a loved one dying, losing 100 lbs, taking a once-in-a-lifetime vacation, having a baby, a cancer diagnosis, or getting a necessary divorce. The big moments of our lives are awesome and worth celebrating and hard and shape who we are, yet they are fleeting.

We live the vast majority of our lives in a string of tiny moments that prepare us for what's to come and that lead up to the big moments. These tiny moments are what I revere. I revere them because, no matter how small, I believe they are significant.

The decision to take a deep breath rather than panic is significant. To rest for 20 minutes instead of tidying my bedroom. To write for 30 minutes even though it has been a long day. To check in with my friend today rather than wait until tomorrow. To take the time to cook a nice meal for myself, rather than snack and cobble something together that feels unsatisfying. To keep working out even when I want to quit.

The tiniest of moments are the most important because they prepare me for the bigger moments. I can't become successful at lifting 50 lb weights if I don't first start with 3 lbs and work my way up. I can't have a wonderful relationship 16 years in if I haven't been trying and learning and growing most days.

When I'm paying attention to the tiny moments and how I *respond* to them, I'm ensuring that I build a life that is my own—not someone else's. If I continuously make small choices based on what other people think (sometimes without even realizing it), my life is going to look a heck of a lot different 10 years down the road. I will be living a life that isn't mine. I'll be making decisions to please other people. I might not even know these people, or I might not even want to aspire to be who they are, yet here I am performing a magic trick, contorting myself to fit in and not stand out, all without knowing it. It's wild and human and scary.

A few years back, I was changing my son's bed the day before we were having a small party for his fourth birthday. One of his fitted sheets is pink. I love pink on boys and this sheet was leftover from my mum's spare bedroom in France where my nieces used to stay. I was putting the pink sheet on his bed and this thought popped into my mind: *What if someone judges me for the pink sheet? Will they think it's weird? A boy with a pink sheet?*

That thought came out of nowhere as most thoughts do. I immediately caught the thought and was able to ask myself, *What do I think?* I quietly answered, *I love the sheet, and it's cool with me.* I remembered that what others think is none of my business.

This moment sticks with me as such a great example of living in the tiniest of moments. Think about how many moments like this we experience in any one day. Does it matter if I change the sheet because I'm worried about what other people think? Not really. After all, it is a tiny decision that is relatively inconsequential. Over time, though, leaving these thoughts unchecked adds up.

Making decisions consciously is the difference-maker. I could decide to choose a different sheet because I don't want to deal with the potential for someone else's judgment. That's ok. That's honest. I would also want to circle back to that thought and understand what has me so emotionally charged that I'm struggling with the color of a fitted sheet.

Let's be clear, it isn't about the pink sheet. You might say, "Sarah, what are we talking about here? Who cares? Put the sheet on, or don't. It's insignificant when you have so many other things to take care of." In response, I say, "I agree … *unless* a thought like this represents a pattern of second-guessing yourself and living your life for other people." If it means you can't get in tune with your fears and desires, then this pink sheet scenario is the whole enchilada. This is the work right here.

If I can't catch the fact that I even had this thought and then make a conscious choice to prioritize the question *What do I think?* over insidious gender norms, I don't have a shot at shaping my life in the way I want to shape it. How could you respectfully disagree with your boss's opinion on a project if you can't have a hard conversation with yourself in the tiniest of moments?

If you react to a tiny moment by saying, "Oh, it's nothing," you might be devaluing your feelings. I tend to say, "I know it's small but/and …" (The "but" still creeps in in this context.) I am committed to catching myself and changing this language. To understand that I am worried about what other people think about the pink sheet and to course correct is not a small thing.

I find referring to things—a career opportunity, a new relationship, a clean house—as "big" or "small" to be troublesome because I struggle with self-worth. I don't want to get ahead of myself or minimize an accomplishment. I'm always working to find an equilibrium between who I am and how I feel about myself. "Big" can be a clue that I'm trying to be grandiose or make a moment bigger than it is to make *myself* feel bigger. "Small" hints at insignificance, which is a representation of how I can feel insignificant.

What feels more true is that all moments are *important*. I want to feel proud and moved any time I can catch my words and behaviors and make an adjustment. It's a life-changing skill that creates a snowball effect.

As your coach, I'm going to celebrate your tiny wins over and over because they build belief and confidence, and they are worth celebrating. Who doesn't want to celebrate? We could all do with a lot more celebration in our lives. Especially when it comes to pink-sheet moments.

I encourage you to celebrate all your tiny moments instead of awkwardly making them small. You are only as small as you imagine yourself to be. I am only as small as I imagine myself to be. Let's not shrink ourselves in the name of living someone else's life.

Words Matter

I have always loved words. I wasn't an avid reader growing up. I'm still not, and I like to read. I remember doing the crossword with my parents, looking up the meaning of new words in the dictionary, playing spelling games, and having an advanced vocabulary as a child. I also liked accents and had a small knack for imitation, which I enjoyed practicing.

I loved to stand up in the classroom and read aloud. I was once praised by the Deputy Headmistress for my reading-aloud abilities. For me, the gift of pronouncing words with clarity and accuracy is heavenly. I don't like to stutter or misjudge even one word. This is certainly a call out to perfectionism on my part. Words don't have to be pronounced accurately or stated perfectly to convey something that moves us.

I delight in pronouncing a word just as she is, in savoring the sound and shape of a word, making connections between words, and acknowledging the rhythm of the sentence as outlined by the punctuation. When I was learning Spanish, discovering the meaning of a new word and learning how to say it in a way that a native would say it made me giddy. I didn't want to say something well enough to get by. I wanted to master the art of self-expression that matched the thinking, feeling, and experiences of Hispanic people.

I equate part of language learning to mathematics. While there is an art to expressing oneself in a different language, the formula for conjugating verbs feels more scientific, more exact. I never excelled at or enjoyed maths, but verb endings were a delight and made sense in my brain.

It's no coincidence, although I only made this connection much later in life, that I went on to study languages at university. To my surprise, my foray into coaching wasn't the huge departure from languages that it seemed to be on paper. As I developed my rhythm as a coach, I found myself being drawn to words. Not just for the sound and structure this time but because our words matter. Our words represent our feelings and our thoughts. Our words inform our actions, and our actions determine our outcomes and our reality.

What we say impacts the course of our lives, and I wanted to help my clients understand this correlation. We can be lazy with our words, and we can be disciplined with our words. And beyond the words themselves, what we're really searching for is the truest nature of our expression. To know who we are and communicate that knowing with clarity. To represent ourselves honestly. I want to master the art of self-expression that matches *my* thinking, feeling, and experiences.

A favorite teacher of mine, renowned Sports Psychologist and Mental Conditioning Coach Trevor Moawad (who sadly passed away from cancer in his early forties in 2021), taught about the power of neutral thinking. You might be surprised to know that there isn't a lot of science supporting the power of positive thinking. There is, however, a lot of data to support the harmful impact of negative thinking.

What's most interesting to me, and what Trevor taught many top athletes and teams across the globe, is the power of neutrality. When we remove negativity *and* positivity and focus instead on being neutral, we experience superior results. I gobbled up this perspective because I have always felt a little averse to positivity as a solution.

Here's where this information gets really interesting. Trevor says that negative thoughts are four to seven times more powerful than positive ones. If you say something negative out loud, it is 10 times more powerful than if you simply think it. To put that into everyday context, if I'm saying things like, "It's so hot," "Ugh, I'm so tired," or, "Our world has gone to shit," I am multiplying the likelihood of those outcomes becoming my reality by 40-70 times.

I know.

Please believe me when I say words matter.

I do believe there can be value in indulging our negative thoughts. Acknowledging them to understand our current situation so we can have a better roadmap for the future can be helpful and necessary. Simply permitting ourselves to wallow in self-pity—to be sad, vengeful, depressed, or any so-called negative emotion—is vital. We are supposed to feel all of our feelings. Sometimes they are the only fuel and protection we have when life feels like it's falling apart.

The difference maker is that we don't want to stay in these negative emotions for any longer than we need to.

Trevor's recommendation to remain neutral helps to raise our vibration and reminds us to not complain about the small stuff that doesn't matter. Magic doesn't happen when we're living in fear, insecurity, or rage. Magic happens, flow happens, and miracles happen when we feel content, optimistic, passionate, and free. Our choice of words can position us there.

Brené Brown

Someone recently said to me, "I know it's cheesy, but Brené Brown is my girl." I thought for a second and then said, "There's nothing cheesy about that statement. I love Brené."

How could it be cheesy to have been moved by someone? How could it be cheesy to cherish someone who is doing great work in the world?

Brené Brown changed my life. I read her book *Daring Greatly* and couldn't believe what I was reading. I gobbled up every line. I memorized sections from it for my first speaking gig. I share passages from it in my retreats. I introduce people to the book. I make it mandatory reading for some of my clients.

In short, Brené laid out the framework for an emotional landscape that I craved and didn't know existed. Brené gave my deepest desires and fears a new language. After reading that book, I came to understand that we didn't do vulnerability in my family.

When I was 14, my pony, Raffles, who I adored, suddenly died. I had ridden him almost every day since I was nine years old. He was my best friend. Raffles was having a routine vaccination, and a new young vet didn't realize that the double dose that he thought was standard was actually an overdose. Shortly after receiving the second dose, when I went to catch him in the field to ride him as usual, he was wheezing and clearly in distress. Within a few hours, he was dead. I was sent down to the neighbor's house so I didn't hear the gunshot that was standard practice by the vet to put him to sleep.

The night that Raffles died, I was supposed to be going to a "ball," which was a black-tie party for teenagers. My mum strongly encouraged me to go because she thought it would be good for me and take my mind off what had happened. So I went.

As a family, we didn't know how to sit down and mourn. To cry uncontrollably for such a sad loss. To feel the appropriate feelings when your heart is broken and in shock. The disease of alcoholism will do this to a family. Instead, we moved forward. I went to the party and spent most of the evening seemingly boasting, telling people that my beloved pony had died. I liked the shock and awe of saying such a thing. What's more true is that I didn't know how to channel my feelings about this unbelievable event.

Vulnerability? I had no idea what that was. Through reading Brené's works, I could see it was the thing I was desperate for. I still am. Per Brené, the definition of vulnerability is "uncertainty, risk, and emotional exposure."[6] Logically, I don't want to live at risk, full of uncertainty, and emotionally exposed. Not at all. It doesn't sound fun. And I also know that I need to experience what it means to feel vulnerable to embody my full human experience. I want to learn how to let my guard down, to breathe, and to feel close to people. I want to feel alive and at peace, and that requires embracing vulnerability.

The message in *Daring Greatly* that still gets me to this day is this: the only way we can experience joy is through the practice of vulnerability. *What?* When Brené asked research participants about the experiences that left them feeling the most vulnerable, they answered with stories about joy. Not fear and shame. *Joy.* They described moments such as standing over their child while they're sleeping, loving their job, going into remission, and falling in love.

In the book, Brené writes, "When we spend our lives (knowingly and

---

[6] Brené Brown, *Daring Greatly: How the Courage to Be Vulnerable Transforms the Way We Live, Love, Parent, and Lead*, 1st ed. (New York: Avery, 2015), 34.

unknowingly) pushing away vulnerability, we can't hold space open for the uncertainty, risk, and emotional exposure of joy."[7]

Please read that again. *When we spend our lives (knowingly and unknowingly) pushing away vulnerability, we can't hold space open for the uncertainty, risk, and emotional exposure of joy.*

To this day, I marvel at this revelation. It is the one fact that encourages me to engage with vulnerability every chance I get. Since Brené introduced me to vulnerability, I haven't let it go. It set me on a new path and became the central tenet of my work as a coach.

I realized that I want to help people develop their sense of self. I want to help women especially understand what they are thinking and feeling, so their actions can be more intentional, and their outcomes more aligned. I want them to feel safe enough to take the risks that matter to them. I want them to understand shame. To know that it's the most potent emotion we feel. To know that it thrives in the dark so staying quiet about our struggles isn't a good life recipe. To speak up with greater ease rather than being in a ball of worry and angst. I want to help them say, *I'm struggling.* Or, *I don't know where to go from here,* rather than pretending they have it all figured out.

For a long time, pretending was my crutch. If I was in a conversation with someone, and I didn't quite follow along but I understood the high points and the main thread, I opted for safety. I would nod and smile and say something that kept me engaged enough and looking good. Looking good was the thing I wanted to protect at all costs.

I wanted to ask questions and dig deeper. *What do you mean by that? I haven't heard of that, tell me more. I lost you. Can you walk me through that again?* But I didn't have the courage because I was worri-

---

[7] Brown, *Daring Greatly*, 122.

ed I might look stupid. If someone thought well of me, I didn't have to feel uncertain, at risk, and emotionally exposed. Phew. Vulnerability avoided—or so I thought.

I was trying to outrun vulnerability by armoring up with perfectionism. Brené says that "Perfectionism is, at its core, about trying to earn approval."[8] When I read this line, I squealed with delight. It's rooted in the question, "What will people think?" This was such a full circle moment for me because my favorite question, *What do I think?* lines up as the antidote to perfectionism. It's an example of healthy striving,"[9] or being self-focused. It stands to reason that the only thing I can control is me. When I try to please other people and focus on managing their views of me, I've lost control by inadvertently giving away my power. When I'm too worried about what you think of me to live my life, I sacrifice myself.

Did Brené influence my instinct to latch onto the question, *What do I think?* Since she is such an influence on me, there's definitely a correlation. It was also awesome to realize years later that I was developing language tools of my own based on my life experiences. I felt alignment with my girl, Brené, like a little nod from God that I'm doing well, and that still brings me great joy.

Today, I'm clear that my only job is to be me. If I have a question, I do my best to ask it. If somebody asks me how I am, I do my best to answer honestly with an understanding of the context. If I disagree, I do my best to share my differing point of view rather than laugh along with everyone else.

Even when being myself feels icky and regretful, I find that those feelings aren't the feelings that persist. Yes, they are challenging. What

---

[8] Brené Brown, *Dare to Lead: Brave Work. Tough Conversations. Whole Hearts,* 1st ed. (New York: Random House, 2018), 79.

[9] Brown, *Dare to Lead,* 79.

persists most is a sense of gratitude for trying out who I am, for staying true to what feels best for me in the moment, and for being open to vulnerability. Ten years into this new way of being, I'm clear that the pain of pretending is far greater than the pain of being myself.

Three cheers for Brené.

Vulnerabilities

If you think you don't need to do vulnerability, or that it doesn't apply to you, read these examples of vulnerability. This list is taken directly from Brene Brown's *Daring Greatly*.[10]

She asked research participants to answer this question, "Vulnerability is _____." Here are some of their answers. As you read this list, I want you to think about how often these circumstances present themselves every single day.

- Sharing an unpopular opinion

- Standing up for myself

- Asking for help

- Saying no

- Starting my own business

- Helping my 37-year-old wife with Stage 4 breast cancer make decisions about her will

- Initiating sex with my wife

- Initiating sex with my husband

---

[10] Brown, *Daring Greatly*, 35-37.

- Hearing how much my son wants to make first chair in the orchestra and encouraging him while knowing that it's probably not going to happen

- Calling a friend whose child just died

- The first date after my divorce

- Saying, "I love you," first and not knowing if I'm going to be loved back

- Writing something I wrote or a piece of art that I made

- Getting promoted and not knowing if I'm going to succeed

- Getting fired

- Falling in love

- Trying something new

- Bringing my new boyfriend home

- Getting pregnant after three miscarriages

- Waiting for the biopsy to come back

- Exercising in public, especially when I don't know what I'm doing and I'm out of shape

- Admitting I'm afraid

- Telling my CEO that we won't make payroll next month

- Standing up for myself and for friends when someone else is critical or gossiping

- Being accountable

- Asking for forgiveness

- Having faith

I read this list often to clients and when I'm leading groups, and it takes my breath away every single time. I'm reminded of the fact that vulnerability lives in every corner of our lives. We can't outrun it or escape it. This list reminds me that vulnerability is the very fabric of my life, so I better buckle up and do the hard and beautiful work of understanding myself.

Moving to the U.S.

When I was 19, after finishing my first year of university, my parents decided to sell our house—the only house I had lived in in England—and move to the south of France.

Their decision to move to the south of France came after hunting the length and breadth of the Spanish coastline to try and find a spot overlooking the Mediterranean Sea. My mum had always wanted to live on the water. After coming up short because the coast was too overdeveloped for them, they decided to live on the top of a mountain in the south of France. Flexible is their middle name.

Having been raised with this type of mindset and sense of adventure, I was looking to my next step after finishing university. I was grateful that I studied something I loved (languages and linguistics), and I didn't know what I wanted to do. It was up to me to forge my path.

Many clients that I coach who are in their twenties are dying to know their plan. I introduce them to the idea that the plan is none of their business. Your plan is to develop a deep sense of self-awareness so whatever decision you make next is as intentional and honest as it can be. While it's great to have goals and aim for something, we also have no idea who we are going to be tomorrow, let alone five years from now.

Have a plan and be very flexible in its pursuit.

The south of France, as lovely as it is, wasn't very enticing to me. My parents lived in a very rural area so there weren't any jobs I was interested in, and I didn't want to pursue a life in France or in French.

I decided to move to Liverpool to stay with my sister, Trish, who kindly invited me. If my parents had still lived in my childhood home, which was in a tiny village called Landulph in Cornwall, I know I would have gone there. That one decision by my parents to move to France, leaving me a home base that didn't feel like home, altered the course of my life. Had they not, would I have ever made it to America? Would I be a life coach now? Would my husband be Preston and my child Austin?

It's so interesting to me to think that one decision that someone else makes can affect so much. I don't ask these questions to focus on regret or what could have been. I ask them because I'm reminded that the decisions we make have ripple effects. In that sense, never underestimate the power of your influence.

In Liverpool, I started selling gas and electricity door to door. I loved the experience. I didn't love knocking on people's doors per se, but I did enjoy the challenge. Selling anything door to door is incredibly character-building, especially for a "posh" girl in the largely working-class city of Liverpool. Sometimes I was so scared that I would barely knock on the door so nobody would answer. I loved the people, my boss, and the ability to one day start an agency of my own. I was drawn to the idea of having control over something that was mine. I was a decent salesperson and showed great promise. It was a fun time, and I worked hard.

During that summer, a "cousin" of mine visited my sister from Washington, DC. My sister is technically a half-sister and this cousin is my sister's cousin from my dad's first marriage. Her name is Maria. I had grown up seeing Maria from time to time. She was in Liverpool catching up with her relatives and while at our house for dinner one night she said, "Why don't you come and stay with me in DC?"

Maria was an art teacher and many of her friends at school were language teachers. They had connections with schools in South America, which sounded enticing. Considering the language opportunities in

DC with regard to translation and the Capitol, coupled with a long-standing knowing that I would one day live in the country where I was born, I found myself on a flight two weeks later to the U.S. of A. I was 22 years old.

See, I was born in Tampa, Florida, and we moved back to England when I was three years old for my schooling and to be closer to family. As a result, I have always had dual citizenship between the U.S. and the UK. I'm very grateful for that advantage that I can only describe as privilege and luck. There are so many things we don't choose due to our parent's circumstances.

I asked my parents to buy the one-way plane ticket for me, and I arrived at Dulles International Airport on September 21, 2005, with about $100 to my name, one rucksack, one huge holdall, and a whole lot of optimism. Just like I had learned from my parents, I was flexible and up for the next adventure.

Preston

The day I landed in DC, I secured a hostessing job at an Irish restaurant within walking distance of Maria's house. While eagerly starting my American life, I unexpectedly received a call from my half-brother, an executive in the oil and gas industry who lived in Houston, Texas. Upon hearing I was now stateside, he offered me a job at his company.

To be clear, I did not want it. My recollection is that I said no thank you. He called back a couple of days later saying he had booked me a plane ticket and was excited for me to fly in and complete a training program. I said yes to appease him, completed the training program, and before I knew it, only two weeks into my American journey, I was accepting a corporate job and starting my life in Texas.

One year later, I quit that job and decided I wanted to go back to school to get a master's degree, mostly because it sounded good and I didn't know what my next adult career move could be. I found a degree I liked at Texas A&M University, which was located in a small town called College Station, about 90 minutes away from Houston.

I was excited to start this next phase of my life and ready to embrace all the possibilities. Was meeting an American boy and falling in love at the top of my list? Yes and no. I had never had a boyfriend until I met Preston. While I yearned for a relationship and to break the stigma of not having had one, it was also scary for me to let my guard down. Since vulnerability was still foreign to me, I was constantly sabotaging what could be. I didn't know how to be myself, and I was scared of what could happen if I got what I wanted. So falling in love with Preston was a miracle all by itself.

As I embarked on settling into life in College Station, a string of serendipitous moments followed that brought Preston and me together.

Serendipitous Moment #1

When I went to check out the university and meet with the advisor of my program, I also decided to look at apartments to see what my money could buy me.

I called a company I found online and spoke to a nice lady. Because this was a small town in Texas and I had been living in a nice part of Houston, I believed that the rent would be pretty cheap in comparison. With my English accent, I said that I was looking for a one bed/one bath apartment with a washer and dryer in the unit, a balcony, and an updated complex with a pool. My budget was around $500/month. She put me on hold and, unbeknownst to me, announced to the whole office, "Some girl with an accent is looking for a high-end apartment for $500 a month. Who wants to help her?"

I later learned the going budget for my request was $1,200 because even though it was a small town, it was a college town, which commands higher rents. Clearly, she didn't want to help me. At the very moment she announced my request, Preston was walking through the door returning from another appointment. He said, "She has an accent? I'll help her."

We spoke on the phone and set up an appointment for later that morning. He later told me that even though I sounded hot, he doubted that I'd look hot because never in all his years of real estate and apartment locating had the two come together. That nice lady? Turns out she was (and still is) a close family friend named Aimee, and we still giggle about that call.

Serendipitous Moment #2

When I arrived at the office, we shook hands and said hello. Preston grabbed his keys, and we walked to the parking lot and got into his car. What I have described is as brief as it was. I didn't think anything about him other than we were going to look at apartments together. As we got into the car, Preston said, "It's a shame you're just now coming to A&M because I'm about to leave to go on a study abroad trip."

Preston worked in real estate in the summer and was a full-time undergraduate student at A&M. As he was saying this, I remember looking out the window as I was reaching to put on my seatbelt, and my heart dropped. I immediately thought, *Why is my heart dropping? I just met this guy.*

During those few hours together, I felt as though I'd known him forever. We laughed, chatted effortlessly, and I taught him rude English words. He was a small-town Texas boy, and I was a woman of the world—or something like that. By the end of the apartment tour, I was once again reminded that my champagne taste was a far cry from my meager budget.

As we arrived back at the office, both of us said that we should hang out again. We decided that we would have dinner that night. It was already late afternoon, and Preston was training a new hire. He said he could meet me in a couple of hours, so we agreed that I would wait at the Barnes & Noble down the street. He pointed me in the right direction, and off I went.

Serendipitous Moment #3

While I was waiting at Barnes & Noble, I called a friend who lived in Houston. She was going out that night and invited me to a party. I told her I was going on a date with this guy I just met. As I was describing the situation, I got a little scared of going on the date so I started to talk myself out of it. *I just met this guy. What am I thinking? I'd much rather be with my friend.*

As I walked out of the Barnes & Noble, fully planning to ditch Preston and head back to Houston, Preston pulled up, and we went on the date. That was Thursday, June 29, 2006. We have been together ever since. In case you're wondering, Preston did study abroad for five months, which was incredibly hard for me and a great adventure for him. He left seven weeks after we met.

For me, there are so many moments in our story that make it clear that this is who I'm supposed to be with. Is serendipitous the best word? I don't know. It's a beautiful story and one of my most important.

Español

When I was 16, I accidentally started learning Spanish. I grew up in the countryside, and my only way of getting home from school was in the car with my parents. Our house wasn't on any reliable public transportation links, so I often waited at my mum's work until she finished working to get a ride home.

My mum and a few of her work friends fancied learning how to speak Spanish, so they hired a native speaker to come and give them a group lesson. I decided to join them. It was either that or sit in a conference room by myself for two hours. I enjoyed the class and soon realized I was good at it. It was the beginning of a love affair with all things Hispanic—the music, the films, the food, the people.

I went on to study Spanish at university and was awarded a distinction in spoken Spanish. While I felt very confident in my abilities at the time, I lost my confidence altogether when I moved to America. I had a degree in languages on my resumé, and I felt so embarrassed that I no longer had that going for me.

You may be asking yourself, *What happened?* Me too. Here's what I can put together. Up until moving to Houston and accepting the job in oil and gas, I was gung ho about putting my language skills to work doing some combination of teaching, translating, and writing.

While I had traveled across the world with my family as well as solo and had lots of life experience by the tender age of 22, living in Houston was the first moment that I was truly out of the nest and on my own.

America felt very familiar. This was the country I was born in and had visited many times, and the language was the same. Once I started working and living in Houston, I experienced the biggest culture shock of my life. The values and atmosphere felt conservative, and I felt like a fish out of water. I didn't realize it at the time, but I was learning to make my own way, to furnish my own apartment, to manage my own money, to be an employee, to make new friendships, to build my life. All while being halfway across the world in a city where the only person I knew was my brother, who I wasn't particularly close to.

I'll also add that, at that same time, my parents were on an extended vacation in Australia and New Zealand and largely unreachable. I couldn't talk to the two most important people in my life whenever I needed to. Moving to America sounded fun, and there were many moments that were. That first year was also one of the loneliest and hardest of my life, and it took a toll on my confidence.

Before I got my apartment in Houston, I lived with my brother for a few weeks. He is fluent in Spanish because he lived and worked in South America and he's married to a lady from Venezuela. Much of her family was visiting at that time, and the house was filled with Spanish. At some point, I became aware that my brother was fluent, having picked it up as he went along, and I was not as fluent, having studied it for seven years. That thought unsettled me.

I remember talking to one of the family members in Spanish, and she couldn't understand me. After some back and forth, I remember she, along with others, started laughing at either my pronunciation or a word I was trying to use incorrectly. I wish I could have laughed along with them with a feeling of, *phew, glad we got that figured out.* Instead, I felt as though they were laughing *at me*, and I felt so small. At that moment, already feeling a little unsafe and unsteady in the world, I unconsciously decided that it wasn't safe for me to speak Spanish.

When I decided to get a master's degree, I chose to study Comparative Literature. Comparative Literature is a bit like an English degree except the comparative part requires a second language. Mine was Spanish. I was hopeful about my ability to get on track with my Spanish and still hadn't given up on my dream of doing some combination of teaching, translating, and writing.

Many of my classes were in Spanish. I had to give presentations in Spanish. Somehow I got through it and did well. However, those two years spent studying did not recalibrate my confidence. If anything, I continued to feel so far out of my element that I only hunkered down in the belief that it was unsafe to speak Spanish, and that there was something wrong with me because I couldn't turn my fear around.

There were moments that were excruciating. I would sometimes see a fellow student who was Cuban walking toward me on campus, and I would get out my phone, pretending to answer a call so I didn't have to speak to him. I walked with one of my Hispanic Studies professors several times across campus. I liked her and her classes a lot. I would speak Spanish for a little while to placate her, congratulating myself on the effort, then move to English as quickly as I could. She never took me to task, thank God.

Another of my survival techniques was to wait to comment until literally the last minute of a two-hour class where we spoke only in Spanish … because I was working up the confidence to speak. I desperately wanted and needed to say something. My rationale was that if I waited until the very end of the class there wouldn't be enough time for people to ask questions and for me to explain myself. I felt like a scam.

I would dodge telling people what I had studied. Instead of saying Spanish, I would say linguistics. I dreaded meeting someone Hispanic, especially if someone we both knew said, "Oh, Sarah speaks Spanish." I'd quickly resort to English. In those moments, I wanted to crawl out of my skin and run. It was disconcerting to have been so wonderful at something and to have loved it so much and to now feel like it was a dirty secret I had to hide at all costs to preserve my sense of self.

Logically, I knew that if I messed up when I spoke Spanish, it wasn't a big deal. I could just keep trying. And I didn't know that to be true because it didn't live in my bones. My body felt too unsafe to believe that logic.

To this day, I am still struggling in my relationship with Spanish. I like to keep the subject at bay, and Preston likes to bring it up. I hate it when he tells a native speaker that I speak Spanish. I typically answer by saying, "Hablo un poquito," meaning, "I speak a little," or, "Hace mucho tiempo que no lo hablo," meaning, "It's been so long since I've spoken it," and then I divert straight to English. He tells me he doesn't get it. Neither do I, completely. He doesn't need to get it. Neither do I.

Over the last few years, I have noticed that the grip this story has on me is lessening. I have been brave enough to book a few Spanish lessons that I have really enjoyed, and I have watched several Spanish TV series with English subtitles. I still love the feeling of hearing the language. I still listen to Spanish music, and when I finish this book, I am sure that one of my next goals will be to start group Spanish lessons. I have already identified an organization that specializes in helping learners regain their confidence. I am sure that my time is coming to rewrite this story.

My journey with Spanish has been a long one and a hard one at times. I feel like I lost a part of myself. I also believe the experience of writing my book is teaching me how to let go of my judgment toward myself and to embrace my reality so I don't have to keep running. Instead of feeling tight and unsure when anything Spanish comes into my purview, I am starting to remind myself that I'm scared and that it's ok for me to be scared. I don't have to be ashamed or embarrassed because I'm scared or because I have two degrees in Spanish. I can accept what is—and I must if I am to heal.

Losing my confidence in Spanish was the perfect storm of life events that I'm slowly unwinding. This is my journey, and we all have experiences that keep us from feeling like ourselves. What I want more than anything is grace. I trust the whole process, and estoy emocionada para lo que viene (I'm excited for what's to come).

Al-Anon

I have been a member of Al-Anon Family Groups, a 12-step program for friends and families who have been affected by the disease of alcoholism, since I was 25.

Please don't miss what I'm about to say. Addiction is often referred to as a family disease. If the word disease makes you uncomfortable, think of it as dis-ease. Some people have a hard time with diagnoses or labels, and almost everyone can identify with a sense of dis-ease or discomfort with their emotions or within their family.

What most people don't see is that everyone around the alcoholic/addict is playing a part in the dysfunction. The family members are the do-gooders, the ones cleaning up their messes, fixing everything, and trying to keep the family together. When a family member fixes a situation, they inadvertently prevent the addict from hitting rock bottom, which robs them of the dignity of experiencing their journey.

Hitting that lowest point might be exactly what they need to change, and swooping in to help only enables the addict's behavior. While we have the best of intentions wanting to "help" (in the program we say that helping is the sunny side of control), an addict, or anyone for that matter, needs to feel the consequences of their actions.

It's easy to point a finger at the addict or alcoholic because they are the ones making the poor choices. Their terrible behavior is obvious: falling down drunk; stealing; hiding bottles; showing up late for work; lying; losing a job, home, and relationships; illness; infidelity; perfectionism. Pointing the finger is a symptom of the disease of a family member. Common thoughts include ... *You're the issue. If only you'd stop drinking, then everything would be ok. Why are you ruining our lives?*

Here's what I'll tell you from a combined 35 years in recovery between me and Preston. The issues seldom stop when the alcoholic stops drinking. They may temporarily subside, and life may seem a little easier—until the feelings of being irritable and discontent soon rise to the surface once again.

You see, the drink and the drug are but a symptom. Picking up a drink and taking a drug—such as overeating, overspending, sex addiction, and being controlling, among many other dysfunctional behaviors—are coping mechanisms. The true, underlying issue is the addict's inability to deal with the thoughts, feelings, attitudes, and behaviors around inadequacy and self-worth. And, to boot, every family member experiences the same challenges, too. That's what unites us all in the alcoholic home. That's why addiction is a family disease.

I walked through the doors of my first Al-Anon meeting full of inadequacy. Like many Al-Anon members, I didn't go to my first meeting for myself. Many newcomers to Al-Anon come because they want to learn how to stop a loved one's drinking. Preston was already five years sober when we met. I went because "we" were having problems, and Preston suggested it might help. Are you catching this? I went to Al-Anon even though he wasn't drinking.

I also went because I wanted to make him proud. Said another way, I wanted the praise. I wanted to hear that I was a good little girl for going, for doing the right thing. Now that I'm writing this, it occurs to me that I have always loved being praised. I have lied and still lie to receive praise. I might say that it is one of my drugs of choice.

This may sound odd, calling a feeling a drug of choice. Another 12-step fellowship, Adult Children of Alcoholics and Dysfunctional Families (ACA), attracts members who want to address their addictive relationship with feelings and emotions—just like alcoholics who address their addictive relationship with alcohol and drugs. These feelings include being addicted to stress, fear, anxiety, depression, anger, elation, and disappointment. Interestingly enough, they refer to their relationship with these emotions as the inner drugstore in an effort to understand what is going on inside the body when they arise. I can certainly relate to being addicted to feelings.

The best way I could describe my feelings of inadequacy is that nothing ever felt like enough. Preston and I would go on holiday, and I would end up in tears on the way home because of something Preston said. Or, I would feel disappointed because it wasn't the perfect vacation. I didn't know the perfect vacation doesn't exist and that a vacation won't fix the way I feel and make me automatically happy.

We would argue about who knows what. When Preston finally said what I wanted him to say, I'd find a new reason to continue the fight. Getting him to say what I wanted him to say didn't satisfy my distress at all. I once heard an Al-Anon speaker say, "I made him jump through a hoop, then I made the hoop smaller, then I set it on fire."

Newsflash. These disappointments and fights had nothing to do with Preston and everything to do with me, and I didn't know that. I thought he needed to change so I could feel better.

The first meeting I went to was on a Tuesday evening in September 2008 in Houston. I was scared and unsure. Could it be a possible solution for my constant struggles—my dis-ease? I cried for 55 minutes of the hour. I heard somebody say the word "dad," and I was a goner. My dad was the drinker. I don't remember anything else about that meeting except that a lovely woman named Carol consoled me.

I went home, eager to please and be praised, and I got exactly what I wanted. I don't know why I went to my next meeting, and my next one, and my next one. I can say that the people were describing what I felt, and I felt better walking out of those meetings than I did walking in. There were a lot of weird things that I didn't understand, like tra-

ditions and business meetings and God and slogans and group con-
sciences. No mind. They weren't nearly as important as understanding
myself and my pain.

In time, I came to understand these aspects of the program, and I'm so
glad I wasn't deterred by the unknown. It took me years and years to
speak up confidently, and I spoke up anyway. It took me years and
years to understand my perspective of who God is. Like anything, my
program has been a process.

As I write this, I celebrate 14 years in Al-Anon. I am so thankful for
them because they have changed my life.

Only when the pain is great enough do we become willing to change.
I believe that my pain was great enough to keep me going back to Al-
Anon. Something had to change, and my pleading and performing
were leaving me with no clear answers. Nobody can measure how great
the pain needs to be in order for change to occur. That's the part that
is so difficult, so gut-wrenching—especially when a loved one is suffering. And yet, getting out of the way and helping ourselves is the best
way to help them. It seems counterintuitive, I know.

On that note, the best way you can help your child who is struggling
with mental health and addiction issues is to help yourself. Model the
behavior you wish to see in them, so your family can change its patterns. If one person changes, everyone changes because you're no
longer all doing the same dance. Don't change with the expectation
that *they* will change. Commit to changing yourself because you understand that you are part of the problem, too, and that this is a family
disease. A child learns dysfunction at home after all. This is no reason
to beat yourself up, and I'm certainly not saying that your child's struggles are your fault. I am saying to focus on what you can control, which
is yourself, and watch the miracles that can occur.

This approach applies not only to active addicts but to any relationship. How often have you wanted to change someone else's behavior because it gets on your nerves? Exactly. Change you, change them.

While I didn't go to my first Al-Anon meeting for myself, *I keep going back* for myself. I am clear today that this program is for me. It curbs my desire to control, perfect, please, and perform. It helps me come home to myself, detach with love, and find the peace to understand who I am and let others be themselves. As Preston would say, "I don't need you to change to be happy." I am learning that I don't need anyone to change to feel at peace.

Al-Anon brings me closer to God because, as it says in the first step, "We admitted we were powerless over alcohol and that our lives had become unmanageable." I am powerless over almost everything, including many of my thoughts. I don't have any active alcoholism in my life today—my dad got sober at 73 years old—and my life still feels regularly unmanageable. I revert to overthinking, worrying, managing, and controlling, especially when I feel stressed. I keep working my program because I want a daily reminder that serenity is an option. The difference today is that I have the tools to catch my stinking thinking a lot quicker than before being in the program. The serenity prayer says it best …

> *God, grant me the serenity*
>
> *To accept the things I cannot change,*
>
> *Courage to change the things I can,*
>
> *And wisdom to know the difference.*

The consistent work that I do in Al-Anon has saved my life and my marriage.

If you or someone you know is suffering because of someone else's drinking, go to Al-Anon and Alateen Family Groups to find a meeting near you: al-anon.org

If you think you have a drinking problem, visit Alcoholics Anonymous for more information and to find a meeting near you: aa.org

Other FREE support groups include:

Narcotics Anonymous (NA): na.org

National Alliance on Mental Illness (NAMI): nami.org/home

Co-Dependents Anonymous (CoDA): coda.org

Adult Children of Alcoholics and Dysfunctional Families (ACA): adultchildren.org

Overeaters Anonymous (OA): oa.org

Sex and Love Addicts Anonymous (SLAA): slaafws.org

Argentina

When I was 20, I lived in Buenos Aires, Argentina, as part of my study abroad program. Most of my peers studied in Spain because it was very convenient to the UK. But I wanted to go to South America. My parents met in South America, and I have memories of getting letters from my dad, telling me of his work adventures rounding Cape Horn, the southernmost tip of the continent. It seemed like the perfect time to live out this dream. A friend from university agreed to go and with *Go for it* running through my veins, off we went.

We flew into São Paulo and waited overnight in the airport to fly into Rio de Janeiro the next morning. A man tried to convince us to leave the airport and see the city with him. My friend wanted to go, but I was adamant that we were staying put. My extensive traveling experience told me that this man was not to be trusted. To this day, I still believe we could have been trafficked or God knows what.

We explored all Rio had to offer, including the infamous Ipanema Beach. My dad once called my mum from Ipanema, and when she asked where he was, my dad looked vaguely at the sign and then said, "I Panama." After a moment, my mum said, "Do you mean Ipanema?" and they both fell about laughing at my dad's ignorance despite being a world traveler. Over the years, we have laughed at that story so many times around the dinner table, and there I was in Rio, seeing the same sign and beach as my parents long ago.

After Rio, we spent an unforgettable weekend in Buenos Aires before going to stay with a host family in Montevideo, Uruguay. Uruguay was to be our permanent address for the next six months, and yet I couldn't shake the feelings I had for Buenos Aires. Neither could my friend. The city had captured my heart. The men were fantastically good-looking, the pace was electric, and the architecture was beautiful. I even fell in love with Las Madres de Plaza de Mayo, a group of women who marched every week in front of the presidential palace, The Casa Rosada, in the name of their disappeared children during the military dictatorship. The connection I felt to their pain and protesting in those first few days lived on with me and became the focus of my master's thesis many years later.

Montevideo, in comparison, felt slow and behind the times. I wasn't enjoying the classes at the university and life lacked the oomph that Buenos Aires had hit me with. Initiated by me, we packed up and left for Argentina. We found an intensive Spanish school to enroll in and jobs teaching English to business professionals, and we rented a gorgeous apartment. We could have stayed in Uruguay. It would have been easier, although not nearly as rewarding.

Our host family was relying on our rent (the equivalent of $600/month for both of us) to pay for their son's tuition at Oxford University in the UK. It was hard to let them down, and the right thing to do for us. I believe we paid them two months' rent in good faith. I called our university and confirmed that our change of plans fit the requirements of our study abroad. And just like that, we were off on our more aligned adventure. I'm often the first to spearhead change, and I'm so proud of my trailblazing abilities.

Argentina won me over. *Mi querida Buenos Aires.* My beloved Buenos Aires. When Preston went on his study abroad soon after we met, he also spent time in Argentina and loved it. We have a dream of splitting time between Buenos Aires and Ohio. Our goal is to test out this dream, 20 years on, to see if it still pulls at our heartstrings.

Charlotte

I have two half-brothers and two half-sisters. I tell most people I am an only child because it feels true. My siblings may feel differently about my answer, and that's ok. I didn't grow up in the same house as any of them. The closest to my age is nine years older than me, and the oldest is 18 years my senior. They have been varying degrees of kind to me, and I've experienced some pain in these relationships, too.

There were many times as a young person (teenager into my early twenties) when I felt harshly judged by my siblings for my misgivings. At times, it felt like I had four parents and that they had forgotten what it was like to be young. I also acknowledge that I had a part to play in some instances, and I take responsibility for my actions.

My greatest ally was my cousin, Charlotte. We are four months minus one day apart (Charlotte is older). She lived about 30 minutes away for most of my childhood. We played and had sleepovers. We tramped through the marsh and woods behind my house for hours. We got stuck in the mud when the tide went out and came home filthy. We enjoyed picnics at various parks. We sat on the wall by the river with our boombox, blaring Whitney Houston, talking about who we wanted to be when we grew up. We went out clubbing, we met boys, we went shopping together, and we got drunk.

Charlotte matured more quickly than I did. She moved out of her home and rented a flat when she was 16. She was working full-time at a Greek restaurant, going to college, and paying her way. She wore more makeup and dated older guys. I was still at home, feeling a little immature in comparison, a bit more straight-laced, and like I didn't fit in with her crowd.

The lie I believe about myself, which I learned in a recent breathwork session, "There is something wrong with me," was clearly already in play. Emotionally, it's hard to challenge that thought, even though, logically, I know nothing is wrong with me. Feeling separate has been a feeling I've had my whole life. How I would have loved to believe in myself, that little bit more, so there wasn't this feeling of separation between us.

Charlotte and I parted ways for many years. We didn't have a falling out, our lives just moved in different directions to different parts of the world. When we reunited three years ago, Charlotte revealed I had written something hurtful about her a few years prior. I had written a card to our maternal grandma, whom we both spent a lot of time with growing up, shortly before she died. It read something to the effect of, "Thanks for saving me from Charlotte for all those years." Charlotte had been cleaning out Grandma's house after she passed away and came across it.

I don't remember the card specifically, and my words immediately rang true. Since I want to be the best, I could imagine wanting to make myself superior to Charlotte in Grandma's eyes. Thanks to Charlotte's courage and honesty, I was able to apologize and be honest, too.

I'm proud of Charlotte for sharing her truth and giving us the chance to become close again, and I'm proud of myself for listening. I'm proud that I didn't laugh it off or pretend it was something else. I got the chance to practice integrity and feel the joy of that alignment even in the midst of an uncomfortable moment. I am beyond thrilled that Charlotte and I reunited.

This story reminds me often that I don't know how my actions affect others. It also reminds me to speak up when I'm the person on the receiving end of something hurtful. I'm grateful that Charlotte reached out to me because I love Charlotte dearly. When I think that I don't need people, I'm just plain wrong. It's a belief that is changing. I need

Charlotte. I want Charlotte in my life.

I'm in the U.S., and Charlotte lives in Wales, in the UK, and while there is a big ocean between us, my heart feels anything but separated. We usually talk multiple times a week, and she is like the sister I maybe wanted. I say maybe because I still think being an only child is pretty awesome. I think I got the best of both worlds. An only child and a sister-cousin exactly the same age. There is no substitute for that history.

Two of my favorite authors, Brené Brown and Glennon Doyle, both have tight-knit connections with their sisters. I often think that I would like to have what they have. And then I remember that I have Charlotte.

Religion

When I was a younger person, I would state with great joy and conviction that religion is a crutch for the weak. I was raised to stand on my own two feet and to keep moving forward, so this statement—this belief system—made sense to me. Like everything, I didn't know what I didn't know.

Until my mid- to late-twenties, I was agnostic. When I joined the 12-step fellowship of Al-Anon Family Groups, I learned that a central premise of the program is a relationship with a Higher Power. Steps one, two, and three from the Big Book of Alcoholics Anonymous are as follows:[11]

> **Step One** - *We admitted we were powerless over alcohol and that our lives had become unmanageable.*
>
> **Step Two** - *Came to believe that a power greater than ourselves could restore us to sanity.*
>
> **Step Three** - *Made a decision to turn our will and our lives over to the care of God as we understood Him.*

Like many newcomers, I had a hard time hearing the word God, let alone developing a relationship with them. Can we talk about pronouns for a moment? I still have much to learn in this area. "He" is the pronoun that most naturally rolls off my tongue when I refer to God.

---

[11] "The Twelve Steps." Alcoholics Anonymous. Accessed February 21, 2023. https://www.aa.org/the-twelve-steps.

However, it feels incomplete. "She" doesn't feel right to me either.

The pronoun "they," while cumbersome for me, feels the most accurate. That God would be a mix of man and woman, masculine and feminine, that the Earth needs both of those energies, that we all have both energies inside of us. That feels true, more complete. With that said, I still feel clunky saying "they" because I feel I would have to explain myself, and I don't want to. I know I don't *have to* explain anything. Maybe that's part of my unlearning.

I believe that Al-Anon was founded on the principle that our self-will and knowledge will only get us so far and are often the source of our suffering. Entering this spiritual program opened me up to the idea of something greater than myself. One of the things I love most about getting older is the gray. When I was younger, I saw things as very black or white, this or that, in or out, right or wrong, for or against.

Even though my humanness has a penchant for certainty, I don't crave it like I used to. I like the allure of it, trust me. I wish things could be certain and clear. And, I know that's not where the magic lies. The gray allows for nuance, for differences, for doubt, for adventure, for, *I don't know.* That's the magic.

It's often said that the last four words of step three in Al-Anon, "as we understood Him," are perhaps the most powerful in the whole program. Al-Anon, like Alcoholics Anonymous, is a spiritual program, not a religious one. This wording creates the freedom to choose a God that makes sense to each of us. God can be anything we can imagine them to be.

As we say in the 12-step rooms, my best thinking got me here. In that vein, I became willing to imagine that my way wasn't working too well and that a relationship with God could be possible for me. While I had a sense that magical things happen—like how I met Preston—I didn't yet associate them with God. I also didn't believe in coincidences. I did, however, perceive there to be something greater than me because I believed my fellow members when they talked about their spiritual experiences. I took stock of how they moved through the world and who they were showing me to be.

It took a decade of me trying out the word God with myself before I felt comfortable saying it out loud and trusting it.

Remembering that God exists, let alone turning over my will to them, is a moment-by-moment experience. I remember, I forget. I remember, I forget. I know my body never forgets. My mind does. Sometimes I'm not sure where God lives, who they are, and how to explain them. Other times, I'm in the spiritual zone, and I don't have to explain a thing because God is in the palm of my hand. For me, God is more of a feeling than a person.

Now and then, I feel uncomfortable imagining that when I use the word "God," you will judge me in a certain way. You will judge me in the ways *I* have judged people who love God: conservative, bible-thumping, can't-think-for-themselves kinda people. It's so interesting to me that what I think you might think of me is what I have thought about you. That loop hasn't yet ceased to fascinate me.

I try to remember that what you think about me is none of my business. When I can give you the grace to be who you are, I'm *magically* not so worried about what you think of me.

Today, I proudly say that I love God. My practice is to keep saying God, without explaining myself, especially when I feel uncomfortable. One million people could say they are followers of God, and we could all mean different things. The cool part is that when I say I love God, I don't have to fit any mold other than what makes sense to me.

Adventures

One of my favorite questions to ask at bedtime as a child was, "Where are we going next?" It was second nature to wake up in the middle of the night, drive to London, and then fly somewhere like Singapore, the Shetland Islands, or Holland. We caught ferries to Spain, walked around The Parthenon in Athens, and ate Greek salads in Piraeus. We rented sailboats in the former Yugoslavia and the Caribbean.

I've been chained to the edge of a boat so I didn't go overboard during a violent storm and hauled up the side of a massive tanker in a wicker basket while anchored out at sea. We visited Saint Lucia before anything was there and saw the twin peaks. We spent several weeks in Baku, Azerbaijan, and a few days with one of my dad's colleagues, Mortaz, at his family's summer home in the Caucasus Mountains. Mortaz's family had lost almost everything when the Russians invaded. I slept on tufts of wool and went to the bathroom in a hole in the ground. I was 12.

When I was at home, my pony, Raffles, and I won cups galore at local show-jumping competitions. I was on a fencing team and placed eighth in a national competition. Yes, fencing as in swords. I played the piano from ages four to 18, and I was awarded my Grade 8 certificate—the highest you can achieve unless you become a professional—by the Associated Board of the Royal Schools of Music. I loved to come home after school and play the piano. It was a great stress reliever.

We lived in a quintessential chocolate box English cottage that we were constantly redoing. It was beautiful. Though I struggled to keep friends, it's important to note that I have endless good memories with them, too. I remember going to Alton Towers, a theme park, for my

10th birthday with two friends and staying two nights. Another friend surprised me with a treasure hunt around her neighborhood when I went to her house. After school, I would often go to another friend's house who lived nearby.

We were close to my mum's side of the family and would drive up to Burnley, a town in northern England, to see them. We would spend a long weekend or a week exploring, chatting, and shopping. We would go to London, where I would get treated to great clothes from posh shops. We loved going to the theater in our local city, Plymouth, and enjoying dinner before or after. All in all, I had a very privileged and delightful childhood.

Go for it really is fitting for how we lived, and as I heard my mum tell Preston just yesterday, we never planned anything. While my head loves a plan to stave off uncertainty, my heart craves adventures. My idea of heaven is coming across an idea or opportunity that makes no sense (or all the sense, depending on how you look at it), which leaves me giddy, and that could happen on a moment's notice. For me, that is a way of living that is the stuff of dreams.

At Odds With Our Emotions

I was standing in my apartment arguing with Preston. I don't remember the specifics. I was 23 or 24, about a year or two into our relationship. I was so enraged that I threw a bunch of bananas at him. He ducked, and they hit the wall. The fact that I missed him infuriated my competitive spirit even more. At some point, I think Preston apologized, or, at the very least brought an energy to the situation that calmed things down. And then, without warning or reason, I began arguing about how he wasn't saying just the right thing, and I was worked up all over again.

I often find myself back in that experience, reliving the feelings in that college apartment. I can see the melamine countertops and the loveseat with a cover from Ross that I switched the price tags on so I could pay less, and I can feel the total dissatisfaction, rage, and desperation that lived inside of me. Those feelings are familiar to me today. At the time, I didn't have the coping skills I needed to understand my emotional needs, to be present, to steady myself, to be forgiving, to right my ship. Instead, I was out in open waters, flailing, grasping, drowning in a storm of my own creation, and I had no idea how to change me or it. Absolutely none.

I want to end that reality for people. When we can emotionally self-soothe, we have the keys to the kingdom. I used to get frustrated at my son when he threw a tantrum; yet, as adults, we throw tantrums every day. A toddler's tantrum is a pure expression of emotion. One that I admire. They are expressing their needs the only way they know how. As adults and parents, it's our job to model and teach healthier ways of processing emotions. We're supposed to have better coping mechanisms. But do we really?

A "do as I say, not as I do" approach is ugly to me. Kids are smart enough to sense the discrepancy. How many of us tell our children to stop crying, yet we're dying for permission to have a good cry, to let it all out? We haven't been taught how to regulate our emotions. It's taken for granted that we will somehow figure it out as we go. What codswallop! We are walking around calling ourselves adults while behaving like children. Then we get frustrated with our children for how they behave because we don't have the tools to process and respond appropriately.

I wish every adult in the world could give themselves permission to go into a private, quiet room and thrash around for a few minutes feeling any emotion just a little more deeply. We need to let out what's inside using healthy skills, not beat up the people we love because our shit is coming out sideways. How much better would we all be if we could engage in consistent self-awareness work?

I yearn to not be that little girl in that apartment. I was so emotionally adrift and in so much pain that prolonging arguments was the best I had. That's why I became a life coach. Because there has to be a better option than slinging bananas.

The Eagle

When I began my master's degree, I was offered free tuition if I worked 20 hours a week as a research assistant. This is pretty common in the U.S.—maybe in other countries, too. Still, at the end of my first year, I bet on myself, took out a student loan, and quit. The research position was incredibly boring so the deal no longer felt good.

Having taken some undergraduate creative writing classes as part of my master's, I followed a feeling that felt better. I leaned on Preston's uncle, Don, who had owned a newspaper with Preston's dad, Bubba, for an introduction to the publisher of the newspaper in town, *The Eagle.*

I put together a portfolio (if you could call it that) of writing samples. The first was a story I had written in high school (that was highly praised by my English teacher) about the summer I spent in Azerbaijan. I also included two published travel articles from my time in Argentina. I'm not sure I qualified for the position, and with a little family connection, a cute English accent and face, and a strong desire and ability to write, I was in.

Telling people that I worked at *The Eagle* gave me the same feeling I get from telling people today that I'm a life coach: pride and joy. I couldn't believe that I got to work at the biggest newspaper in town and was getting paid to write.

I became the Special Projects Editor for the advertorial team and loved every minute of it. I was responsible for writing the signature articles for magazines that got inserted into the main paper, such as "House and Home." I edited special publications like *Reader's Choice* and *The George Bush Museum Special,* among many others.

I also wrote advertorials that advertised local businesses every week by telling their stories. I met every kind of business owner and was exposed to so many passions and paths to success. I don't know how effective my writing was at increasing sales. I do know I received a lot of compliments from the business owners about the level of care and detail I infused into their stories. I know I was good at capturing the essence of who they were and, in turn, they were often very grateful because they felt seen and heard.

Helping people to feel seen and heard is now at the root of what I do as a coach. I loved meeting those owners and hearing their stories. It felt like an honor and a privilege and was unknowingly planting the seed for my journey as a business owner. I'll also note that I asked *The Eagle* to pay me $20/hour—the going rate was $12-14—which was what I needed to pay rent and live. I got it!

It's hard to believe I was only at *The Eagle* for one year. It made a lasting impression on my heart. When I started the position, I was also assigned to be the editor of an insert publication called *The Press*. It was described as a small, family newspaper that had been around for a long time and was struggling to stay alive.

My assignment was to write stories about the community and events around town. I also had my own column called "Something from Sarah." I was so proud of that. I can't say my writing was stellar. I once wrote a column about how girls with cankles shouldn't wear strappy shoes because they aren't a flattering combination. *Oh jeez*. Not everything we do is going to be a win. Neither is it supposed to be. I was cutting my teeth and learning how to craft a story.

At the end of my first day, I was at home telling Preston the details of my new role. When I mentioned *The Press*, he couldn't believe it. It turns out *The Press* was the very newspaper his grandfather, William "Fowler" Moore, had started in his garage. When Preston's grandfather passed away, his dad and his uncle went on to run it for many years before they sold it to *The Eagle*.

I knew that Fowler, Bubba, and Don had started and run a newspaper. I didn't know it was *The Press*. Bubba died three years earlier so I had never met the man, the myth, the legend that was Bubba Moore. As the publisher of the main newspaper in town before *The Eagle* showed up, he was well-known and well-liked. Over 1,500 people came to his funeral. It turns out that Bubba had written a column in *The Press* for many years, just like I was about to do.

When I learned this information, I had known Preston for one year. Another serendipitous moment.

Sadly, *The Press* didn't survive. During that year I worked at *The Eagle*, it was printed for the last time with me, the girlfriend of Bubba Moore's son, as the editor. My very last column was a tribute to Bubba—the man who paved the way for me to be a part of his legacy.

This life experience taught me that unexpected magic happens when I'm willing to upset my seemingly good apple cart and follow my instincts.

Travel Writing

When I was younger, I dreamt of being a travel writer. I imagined myself working at *Condé Nast Traveler* and living my best *The Devil Wears Prada* life (the fancy parts, of course). In the final months of my master's, I was submitting job applications to all of the major travel publications, spurred on by the fact that I was writing every day for the newspaper.

I was finding it difficult to get a foot in the door in New York, LA, and San Francisco, where all the major publications were based, from my small town in Texas. After I graduated from my master's program, Preston and I went to Mexico for six weeks. I had plans to write articles about my time there and submit them. Here's the thing: while in Mexico, I had zero desire to write a single article. I wanted to be a travel writer, and I wasn't writing about my travels.

It wasn't laziness or fear. It felt forced. I came home from Mexico feeling bad about myself. *Why hadn't I followed through? Why weren't my ideas coming together?* I figured there was still time, that I could muster up the energy to do it. I didn't know that it was as simple as I didn't want to. I didn't know that I could still call myself a writer and not write these articles. Accepting that I wasn't writing meant that I had to mourn the loss of the dream of being a travel writer. I wasn't ready to give up on that dream because I didn't know what the alternative was.

I love getting older because I am accumulating more and more examples of how dreams can transform in ways I could never have imagined. For example, the way I feel about my profession as a life coach today is just as rich as I imagined calling myself a travel writer to be. Little did I know that I would write a blog for 10 years, and now this book. I still write, just in a different way than I thought I would. I have no desire to be a travel writer, by the way, and no regrets about walking a different path.

What's potent about this story is that being in pain is a process. There's no quick fix or coaching tool that could have stopped me from feeling bad and confused about why I didn't write in Mexico. Time yielded perspective and forgiveness.

And because I've had that experience and many others, along with a consistent self-awareness practice, I can trust and move through similar experiences more peacefully today. I have muscle memory that reminds me that my ideas aren't always the best ideas and that what I think I want isn't always what I actually want. That muscle memory reminds me that something better might be coming and helps me to let go of the plan and be flexible.

This experience truly crystallized the importance of my actions. I am very clear today that my actions speak louder than my words. If I say I want something, and I'm not taking action to move in that direction, I try to remember to smile and know that I need to reexamine what I'm thinking and feeling. I know there is no need to beat myself up.

Typically, one of two things is happening.

One: I'm probably scared, so my words and actions aren't aligning. If I get quiet and realize I still want the thing I say I want, I start working through it with my coach and my Al-Anon sponsor. I need third parties to usher me forward because it's too much to do alone. Or, two: I never wanted the thing. Perhaps it sounded good, and I wanted to take the time to explore it and get it out of my system. That was time well spent, and now I can let go of it.

Today, a new vision is no longer a prerequisite to letting go of an old one. I'm a bit more comfortable in the space in between—the waiting.

Life Coaching

After finishing my master's, I started working for a lingerie company that specialized in custom bra fittings in Houston. I had wanted to open my own bra store since my travel writing dreams were waning. Having a full bust and a small rib cage, I struggled to find a bra that fit, and I thought there was an opportunity for this niche in the market. I was shocked that in America, the self-promoting "greatest land in the world" where I thought you can get anything and everything, good bras and bra fittings were not readily available.

So instead of starting a company, I joined one to learn the ins and outs of the business. We were in the business of changing women's lives. It was a powerful experience and as I grew in the all-women company, what I loved the most was managing and mentoring the women I worked with. I had this innate sense that if I could manage and "coach" the whole employee, rather than putting a large focus on her sales targets, I could understand *her*. To this day, that is what excites me about coaching. I felt that understanding her overall sense of well being and supporting her would make a bigger impact on the success of the business and her life.

Very early into my tenure with the company, I became clear that I did not want to own my own store. I didn't want to be burdened with a brick-and-mortar, and the hours were relentless. I settled into lingerie life all the while feeling unsettled because I knew this wasn't going to be the forever thing. I also didn't know where to go next. I was ready for what might come, and I wasn't actively seeking. I was simply open.

One day, I found myself reading an article about a life coach based in Houston. At point, I had never heard of a life coach, nor did I know that people were making money doing it. It was a lightbulb moment. The more I read the article the more I felt excited. When I was a teenager, I remember saying I wanted to get paid to have intimate conversations. I didn't know what that meant exactly. I knew I didn't want to be a therapist, counselor, or psychologist, and I didn't know the alternative. I now felt a big glimmer of hope that I had found that alternative.

I reached out to the life coach in the article to see if she would share her experiences with me. She was gracious enough to give me an inside look into her business. She talked to me about her approach with clients, how she ran her books and organized her calendar, and she welcomed me into her home from which she ran her practice. The steps fell into place, and I kept following my energy. All the while I was enamored and a little scared. She had started and run a successful talent agency and was branching off into coaching. It was a natural move for her because she was often asked to coach and consult on all sorts of topics due to her extensive business experience and success.

I knew that I possessed a lot of life experience for a 27-year-old, but I hadn't founded a company or even had significant corporate experience. I wondered if I could be a successful coach. That fear grew legs when I started making calls to coaching schools and the governing body of coaching to learn more about how to get started. I learned that many coaching trainees were in their second or third act after an illustrious corporate career. Who was I to think I could coach? Part of me knew I could. Either way, I wasn't ready.

I spent three more years at the lingerie company gaining experience and preparing to take my next step toward becoming a coach. I found a coaching school that I loved that was based in New Jersey, not far from Philadelphia, where I could do a combination of remote and in-person learning. I kept toying with the idea of starting, and it didn't feel right. In those three years, the thought of being a coach never left me.

Then two magical things happened. Eighteen months into my three subsequent years with the company, they asked me to move to … Philadelphia. Secondly, I became sick to the point that I couldn't walk around the block—not even slowly—without feeling exhausted and sweating heavily. I had hives and severe stomach pains. After many, many specialists and misdiagnoses with little to no answers, a doctor I had met once briefly reviewed my chart and said, "Mrs. Moore, I don't know what's wrong with you, but all of your symptoms can be explained away by depression, stress, and anxiety."

I call that doctor my angel. I knew immediately that my body was screaming at me saying, "We're off track here. You know you don't belong at this lingerie company. It's time to be a coach." There is no medical diagnosis for misalignment, yet my body knew. That was a Friday. I handed in my notice the following Monday morning. Two months later, I began my coaching program at the coaching school I had chosen three years earlier when I lived in Houston, which was now 45 minutes from my house in Philly.

When I first started coaching around 2010, and I was networking a lot, I would tell people that I am a life coach. Many, many times, people would say in response, "Oh, cool. What sport?" I'm clear that I was still worried about my ability to be a coach and to be taken seriously at such a young age. As such, I unconsciously created a reality where I had to explain myself and my profession.

If I think that people don't know what coaching is, or that I'm not a good enough coach, then I'll attract people who believe as such. I'll find myself explaining why it and I are important. Was I just attracting the people who didn't know what coaching was? Or did people really not know what coaching was? I don't know.

It's interesting how our thinking and energy around something can influence what shows up in our world. Sometimes I don't even know when an invented story influences my every move. Coaching beautifully digs into that.

Nowadays, I have little explaining to do. Coaching is more mainstream, most people know exactly what a life coach is, and I've evolved in how I see myself.

I love to say, "I'm a life coach." I love the way the words sound. I feel proud to associate myself with those two words because I know they match who I am. I am in alignment. I marvel at what a beautiful experience it is to walk through life feeling proud of what I do, to have found a thing I love so dearly.

I coach leaders at all levels, from women in their early twenties who are brilliant and finding their way to executives responsible for leading large global teams. I also coach women who are entrepreneurs, founders, executive directors of nonprofits, and employees who value working on themselves and want more from their lives. I can tell you that no matter the age, experience level, or salary of my client, every single woman I have coached desires to assert herself more. They also desire to know themselves more intimately so they can lead themselves, their families, and their teams with more integrity and confidence.

I never want to be doing the lion's share of the work inside the coaching relationship. My client needs to be bench-pressing more than me, so to speak. It's the client's life, not mine. That balance doesn't show my lack of care, it shows that I care a lot. My goal is that the session is a catalyst for my client to think, reflect, be, and do until the next session. The more work the client does between sessions, the more growth there will be in the long run and the richer our sessions will be. There will be more to work with, learn from, and dissect. The session is no substitute for doing *the work*. It's a great complement. Practice self-awareness and the art of reflection, and I'll bench-press alongside you forever.

As a coach, I am interested in one thing: I want to help a woman feel full of herself. To find that comfort, I encourage her to get to know herself intimately and to find the audacity to fall in love with who she is. To do so, she has to be able to identify her feelings, fears, and desires. She has to understand how to slow herself down so she is acting with intention. She has to have a relationship with her body since her body is her ally. That's why consistent reflection practices are spiritual. They transform a spirit so much that a woman will change the course of her life and those of future generations.

With a little more knowledge about herself, I support a woman to speak up in all her relationships. I urge her to ask for what she wants, to know that she can disagree respectfully, to tolerate discomfort, and in doing so, to remember that nothing is wrong with the situation or her. I remind her that she isn't responsible for the feelings of others and that she can survive and thrive being her own woman. I support her in developing tools to approach difficult conversations, and in letting go of the familiar patterns of worry, overthinking, and second-guessing herself. I walk her down the path of developing the courage to shape her own life, tiny moment by tiny moment. All the while, she's helping me do the same.

Coaching Industry

There exists every variety of coach you can think of. Business, leadership, health, life, writing, hormone, positivity ... You name it, there's a coach for it. And as in any industry, there is a pecking order.

For example, business coaches command big money because they help their clients grow successful businesses. It's a shame that business coaching gets such a powerful reaction, and life coaching might not. Isn't living and managing your *life* the most important use of your time? You're running the business of your life every day, business owner or not.

I'm very aware that the term life coach can be a pejorative one. It's a term that can be associated with Janet, who was working at a bank on Friday, decided it was time to quit in the name of helping people, and started coaching on Monday. Oh, trust me, this happens. Nobody in their right mind would dare call themselves a nurse had they not received the appropriate training. That's because the training is so complex.

Due to the coaching industry being largely unregulated and the nature of the work, anyone with a desire to help someone else grow can call themselves a coach. I think of myself as a life coach through and through. And when I meet someone for the first time, particularly in a professional capacity, I most commonly refer to myself as a leadership coach. I'm aware that it sounds more professional and elevates the impression of the work I do.

I know that my opinion about myself counts most, and I'm also aware that the term life coach doesn't always conjure up an image of a professional, intelligent woman. For this reason, every now and again, I'll intentionally describe myself as a life coach. I know that my powerful presence can heighten someone's impression of who a life coach can be, and I feel good that doing so can impact my industry one tiny moment at a time.

Our governing body, The International Coaching Federation (ICF), was founded in 1996. That makes our profession a mere 27 years old (as of this book's publication date). While personal development professionals existed before then, the industry itself is young. As a graduate of a great coaching program and someone who is very active in my profession, I used to be a stickler for anyone who called themselves a coach with little to no formal training.

I was uncomfortable because I felt people like Janet were watering down a wonderful profession that was struggling to find its footing. Let me be more honest. I was worried that if Janet called herself a coach … then what did that say about me? Did Janet's lack of training undermine my standing as a professional coach? Could I even call myself a professional coach if the standards are so lax? Part of me worried about the perception of others as I navigated the desire to be taken seriously and to feel serious.

As time has gone on and I have grown, I see the subject of training as less black and white and much more gray. I started to realize that great coaching giants like Tony Robbins don't have coaching certifications and are doing great work in the world. I know that Tony, who trained with some of the greats, and Janet, who became a life coach basically overnight, are two different kettles of fish. There can be a need and room for both.

The greater point is, who am I to say who is worthy of calling themselves a life coach? If someone is helping another to experience positive change, what business is it of mine to worry about what they call themselves? I can wish Janet well and focus on honing my skills.

I greatly admire the work coaches are doing to strengthen our industry through the ICF and other channels. While I have stepped away from active service in these organizations, I know I continue to make meaningful contributions by being a great example of who a coach can be.

That said, I'm now less interested in how people refer to me as a coach because I'm more sure about my worth. I believe coaching to be one of the most noble pursuits in the world. A skilled coach helps guide people home to themselves. And when we know ourselves intimately, which is our responsibility, everyone and everything around us prospers.

Bad Bosses

Many of my clients inadvertently give away their power to their bosses. They try to please them and find themselves resentful when their needs aren't being met. There are a lot of bosses out there who are *not* leaders. But what can you do about that? You have to please your boss even if they don't care about your potential because they are the one who can promote you, fire you, and make your life miserable … right?

Wrong! You are the person who has agency over your life, and nobody has the power to make you feel a certain way. Blaming your boss for your discomfort is the opposite of creating agency for yourself. Stop giving this person so much power, especially if they are incompetent. Stop believing everything they say. If you don't, your boss will have more power than they deserve.

You might retort, "Sarah, I need this job. I can't afford to get fired so I need to tread carefully and play along." You might be right. I don't know your circumstances. I recognize that there is some privilege in telling you to speak up for yourself at the potential risk of creating a more hostile environment, or worse, getting fired. I also believe that if a boss is taking away your power, something needs to change with you. It's time to go back to the basics of self-awareness.

Take some time to get quiet, journal, reflect, or talk it over with someone, and decide what's really going on. Do you need to speak up and share your frustrations? You owe it to yourself and the relationship to be honest so there is an opportunity for change. Please stop being scared of your boss.

It may be that you need to stay in your job and change the way you interact with your boss. Maybe you need to do some acceptance and forgiveness work toward yourself, and them, to keep hold of your serenity. Someone can be a jerk to you and, while it's hard and unfortunate, you can separate yourself from that behavior. You can retain a sense of self and feel peaceful. I'm thinking of Nelson Mandela. He spent 27 years as a political prisoner, and despite being robbed of so much, he did not give away his hope and fighting spirit.

Let's say you have the difficult conversation. You do your personal work to move through the situation with as much accountability as possible, and you're not happy with the outcome. What other options exist beyond that? Maybe you get another job and take a pay cut, and you're twice as happy. That's a choice. Maybe you chase your dreams toward a totally new career because it's something you've always wanted to do. I recognize these are both privileged options, and yet we often get so bogged down with reaching a certain job title or status, or making more money, that we lose sight of what brings us serenity and peace. What's important is being honest about how you feel and what you want.

Look at your boss as an opportunity. Ask yourself, *What is my opportunity in this situation? What are they here to teach me?* Trust me, they are here to teach you something. Use them as a force for good instead of continuing to blame them and point the finger which makes your behavior equal to theirs. If you can't find anything, you aren't looking hard enough. When you look at them through the lens of being your teacher, the world becomes your oyster because you take back your agency.

And, bosses: Let your employees say what they need to say. You can handle it. If you can't, become the person who can because that is the empowering leadership we need. Brené Brown defines a leader as "anyone who takes responsibility for finding the potential in people and processes and who has the courage to develop that potential."[12] A situation has no shot of changing if you're not willing to speak up and be an agent *for* change. I'd suggest that you don't self-coach your way through this scenario and instead find a professional coach or mentor to help you with your approach.

That said, working alongside somebody who sucks the life out of you can negatively impact your whole being. It can feel unfortunate and unfair, and I know it's really hard. Let me gently remind you that nothing is happening *to* you. Your boss's opinions are a reflection of them, not you. We forget that because it feels so personal. If they are a crappy boss and therefore not someone you respect, why would you allow their opinion to be more important than yours? Don't put up with mediocrity from yourself or others because you're scared of working through your feelings and beliefs.

---

[12] Brown, *Dare to Lead*, 4.

Fantasy

Fantasies are a wonderful form of escapism. We need them. We crave them. They have a soft place in my heart because, at their best, they contribute to a life well-lived. At their worst, fantasies hinder my desire to become self-actualized. For all of us, at some point in our lives, our reality does not match the fantasy we created in our minds, and we feel disillusioned.

Imagine going to a new restaurant, and it's not as good as you hoped. How often do you say something like, "I knew we should have gone to our usual spot"? To be clear, you didn't know you should have gone to your usual spot because you didn't know the new spot was going to be bad. Somehow you thought you could predict the future, knowing what this restaurant had to offer. In reality, you wanted to try somewhere new and when your expectations weren't met, you blamed yourself and your decision-making as a way to justify your disappointment.

More than anything I want to *live in* reality. I want to notice how I'm showing up in situations. I want to notice who people are, and who they are teaching me they are. I want to use fantasy as this bold and enticing breeding ground for becoming and wanting more. That's the purest form of fantasy. Not because I need to become more or different in order to be content but because I want to do and be more to realize my potential, dreams, and curiosity.

I have found that my relationships fall apart when I live in the fantasy of who I want the other person to be. More importantly, I fall apart. I don't want to get caught up in fantastical thinking and deny reality.

Here are some fantasies I've had to rewrite:

Fantasy #1: After 16 years together, Preston should know what I'm thinking and what I need.

There have been so many times when I expected something from Preston that I didn't articulate. As a result, I've felt disillusioned about his inability to not know what I need after being together for so long.

Let's say I'm unsure about a conversation I had with a potential new vendor. Something about it didn't sit well with me. Preston asks, "How are you?" I share how I'm feeling and what happened, and he responds lovingly and then walks off. I'm now mad at him because he didn't give me a cuddle when he knows I like cuddles and that I don't like being left alone when I'm upset. This is a real scenario that has happened. I can't make this up. My thinking can be insane yet seem so sane at the same time.

News flash: He doesn't know what I need nor is he supposed to—even after 16 years together. I have to consistently communicate what I'm thinking and feeling, *and* he's not a bad person, or less of a husband, because he doesn't know.

I want to take a moment to honor my husband. I have loved our marriage and felt proud of it even when it's been excruciating. It is a great privilege to be married to Preston Moore. We have had so many tiny moments of laughter and sadness, and everything in between. This has created great intimacy, fun travels, big moves, and growth that only comes with the gift of time. I have been able to thrash around, be unruly, fall way short, and still feel loved unconditionally. Preston has given that kind of love way better than I have.

I feel as though I'm finally growing into what marriage is—what *our* marriage is—because I continue to understand who I am and how to express my thoughts, wants, and needs.

Fantasy #2: You did something I didn't like. Why am I with you? I need to leave.

My experience of marriage is that I went into it not fully knowing who I was. How can anyone know who they are in their twenties? I was naive about what I was getting into. I did it much less consciously than I would have told you I was doing it at the time. I got married because it was the next step on the ladder of life. Subconsciously, I believed marriage would bring me security. What the relationship has done is hold up the mirror for me to see who I really am. It has taken me every minute and counting of the last 16 years to understand that.

Like parenting, long-term partnership is a conduit for magnifying every inch of me, lovely and not so lovely. So when I have a desire to change Preston, that desire is really an invitation to change something in myself. I can butt up against that desire by insisting that Preston changes. What good would that do? It would only create pain and suffering. I can't change him or anyone else. What I can do is get curious and wonder what it is about me that so desperately needs him to change and get busy doing that work.

My desire to connect with people and feel comfortable around them has grown exponentially. I have Preston, who connects with people so naturally, to thank for a wonderfully consistent example of how I can continue to grow.

Preston, as an alcoholic, can be a domineering personality. Sometimes I struggle to use my voice around him because I feel as though he can be dismissive. When I as much as sense that response from him—is it him or me creating it?—I feel powerless and hopeless and mistakenly believe that I need to prove my idea to him in order to feel worthy. Maybe he's just being an ass, and his behavior has nothing to do with me.

What's also true in this example is that Preston is reflecting back to me my unworthiness. Rather than blaming him for how he responds, I can examine my limiting beliefs. Why do I judge his response as dismissive? What other options could there be? Why do I feel powerless and hopeless just because he doesn't agree with me or like my idea? Where else in my life do I feel the need to prove myself? Why?

Preston is mirroring that which seeks to grow and change within me. My job is to keep the focus on me. It's no coincidence that I teach women how to use their voices.

If you had asked me when I got married if it's my responsibility to take care of myself and bring my whole self to the relationship—each responsible for 100 percent, not 50/50, as we often say—I would have wholeheartedly said yes. It sounded good, and I believed it. But I didn't know how to do it yet. My body didn't feel or know that truth.

Now, having lived the day-to-day of partnership for so long, I have embodied this belief. That's why I always say that I don't know something until it lives in my bones. Knowing something intellectually is only a fraction of true knowing. In fact, I believe that if we only know something intellectually, we don't know it at all.

I've felt the urge to leave my marriage many times because of my disillusionment about what marriage is. I thought Preston was the problem, and I have blamed his actions for my lack of fulfillment. I thought marriage was about being saved, about having another person to distract me from looking so closely at myself. I thought Preston was the one doing the saving because it's so much easier that way. I want to be deeply understood and for marriage to automatically mean my life is joyful. I've spent 16 years unraveling the belief that there is a correlation between joy and being saved.

Joy doesn't work that way. My life's work is to constantly save myself by deeply understanding who I am so that Preston can add to an already fulfilled me. That's how my cup overflows.

Fantasy #3: I need to figure it out.

My brain has been the driving force in my life. I have tried to understand things to the point of overthinking, made plans for the worst, run through every possible scenario by talking it to death, and generally lived in a familiar pulse of chaos and drama. Drama is my one-second, go-to place. That instant hit feels amazing. Everything after that is shit. It's not the way. Drama is unsustainable for the kind of life I seek out and live today.

It's inconceivable to me now that I would be able to figure everything out. Talk about pressure. The more work I do on myself, the more I am sure that there's a magical element to life that will work in my favor if I would just get out of the way. Letting go of the need to figure it out requires vulnerability. I don't believe in coincidences. I believe in God. I believe in the Law of Attraction. I believe in flow. I don't believe the fantasy that I have to know everything, come up with a great plan, and work hard in order to feel safe.

Quite frankly, life is boring if it's always up to me. If my hands are strangling the rhythm of life, there's no room for the plan to be fluid, for things to develop and morph and be better than I could have imagined. Slowing down the noise in my brain by engaging my body in the healing process, rather than thinking my way to a result, is the reality I now choose. I like to say, "Let me be a little less competent and a little more vulnerable." I also like to say, "There's nothing to figure out." Preston likes to say, "It's already done."

Pay attention to your fantasies. How might they be hurting you? Are they actually expectations? How might they be preventing you from accepting reality?

Taking Up Space

I was at Austin's kindergarten Christmas concert at school. It was the first indoor, in-person event the school had hosted in two years because of COVID. Performances were two grades at a time to limit exposure. One of the school staff mentioned that a little boy in an earlier performance kept bowing over and over again.

I was smiling thinking how wonderfully confident this little boy must have felt and how marvelously he was soaking up the experience. I said, "How great that he was taking up space." It quickly became clear that the adult thought I was referring to this boy's physical space. She said, "Oh no, he was standing in one spot. He thought that the applause was just for him." I responded with a smile and moved on.

It occurred to me after that interaction that people don't necessarily understand the meaning of the phrase, "taking up space."

To me, it means to feel and enjoy the fullness of your spirit and to share it with others. To be fully you, to live out loud, to be a light in the world. To energetically and physically be a presence in the room not because you're trying too hard but because you live in alignment and with integrity.

It's not about being showy in a way that is forced or put on. For some of us, taking up space means having a big presence. For others, a smaller, quieter presence. Either way, you're taking up space fully as yourself. Our energetic output is attractive because it reflects our authenticity.

Taking up space is an act of humility which is having the audacity to be who God created you to be.

The Oprah Story

I went to Oprah's "You Can Live Your Life Tour" in 2013. Preston was with me. We drove down from Philadelphia to Washington, DC, and had the most remarkable day. At some point while on stage, Oprah said, in that lovely, booming voice of hers, "I yearn to be full of myself."

I don't know if she followed up with, "in the best way one could imagine that phrase," or if that is something I have since added. I love that disclaimer, though, because I think people's initial reaction to those words is often one of distaste. *Ugh, full of herself, who does she think she is? She's conceited, selfish, stuck up.*

And there we have it, the crux of the opportunity, the whole point of this book, and my work in the world. Does the following sound familiar?

It's too dangerous to take up space, so stay quiet and small. Be polite and contain your emotions. Have desires but don't shout them from the rooftops. Don't even dare to whisper them from the rooftops. Know your place. Suck it up and deal with it. Pretend as if you like it. Pretend it was funny. Look sexy but don't be too sexy. Be a great mother, wife, parent, career woman, and housekeeper. For God's sake, stop crying. Speak your mind but don't be a bitch. You're so emotional.

The messages telling us to tone it down and be just the right amount of—confident, skinny, pretty, sexy, outspoken, you name it!—are insidious. Every woman I work with wants to feel more comfortable in her own skin, more assured of her ability to use her voice, and more trusting of herself and her decisions.

Call it confidence, call it self-esteem, call it executive presence ... call it what resonates with you. I personally do not use terms like boss bitch, boss lady, or badass bitch. These words do not work for me. I'm nobody's bitch, and boss sounds like bossy, which women could stand to hear less.

At the Oprah event, a group of people were dancing in the hallway at the end of the day. One by one, with a DJ off to the side, each person claimed their space in the middle of the circle and danced.

They seemed so free.

I wanted to dive in, and I couldn't get my feet to move. I told myself stories like, *Maybe I'm not as good of a dancer as I think I am. Will I look stupid? Will I look cool? I'll go in a minute.*

I never went into that circle.

This experience was a significant moment in my life.

You may be thinking, *It was just a circle, Sarah. Really? You couldn't get into that circle and dance? It's not a big deal. Who cares?*

It was a big deal to me. I walked away feeling frustrated, and I piled on the shame.

We all come face to face with our own version of that circle on a regular basis. Moments where we want to dive in, and instead, we pull back. I have become very attuned to that pulled-back feeling, and I'm not willing to put myself through that angst, which is my cue to get in the ring.

Today, it's not only about the stories in my head. It's about listening to my body. She speaks to me. I understand the pull toward desire. I know when I'm feeling afraid. I know what the aftermath feels like if I can't find the courage to dive in. Taking up the space that is ours is what we yearn for and when we deny ourselves that right, our body speaks up. Aches, pains, trouble sleeping, chronic issues? Remember, your body will always keep score. I recommend picking up a copy of *You Can Heal Your Life* by Louise Hay to learn more about how there is a probable emotional cause for every physical symptom.

I don't want to stress out my future self any more than necessary by choosing to create feelings that will be more harmful than helpful. When I dive in, that knowing, that anticipation of the feeling to come, while sometimes hard to pinpoint, gives me courage. It's a nervous anticipation. It sometimes feels like a "hell no" with a gentle tug toward something. It's tingles and butterflies. It feels like I'm going to wee myself. It's stress. It's, *Oh shit, we're clearly doing this*. It's hard, and it doesn't feel undoable. It's my GPS. It's a whisper, a nudge from God.

Diving in is big and bright and bold and beautiful even when it doesn't look that way to anyone else. It's having the courage to get into the proverbial circle and do what *I* want without regret or shame casting a shadow on my light.

Perfectionism

Perfectionism is a form of armor I safely tuck myself into when I'm trying to outrun vulnerability. When I feel scared and unsure, I revert back to what I know: pleasing, performing, perfecting, and proving.[13] Perfectionism isn't about crossing all my i's and dotting all my t's. It's about trying to please others first and myself second.

Most of us use the word perfect to mean nothing wrong, flawless. As women, we're in the midst of trying to redefine impossible standards that have been imposed upon us. Like … looking a certain way, working a job and being a mum (which itself is a job, by the way), or working for less pay. And if you're a woman of color, the standards are contorted and more impossible still. The only place that perfection lives is in our heads, yet we're constantly talking about it as if it exists in reality.

When somebody gives us a compliment, we try to deflect it because we misunderstand what perfect means. Does a conversation like this sound familiar?

> Coworker: You killed that presentation!

> You: It definitely wasn't perfect. Was that joke I made awkward or what? Oh, and I stumbled at the beginning. It was good, I guess.

Here's what gets me about the word perfect. We're misusing it.

Why can't you stumble over some words and make an awkward joke

---

[13] Brown, *Dare to Lead*, 79.

and still kill a presentation? We women constantly undermine our-selves because we think we have to do everything flawlessly. It's absurd how we feel a sense of lack unless everything is just so.

Let me introduce you to a new definition of perfection that can help you go easy on yourself. My breathwork coach, Juliana Ericson, re-cently shared it with me, and it's exactly what I hadn't been able to articulate myself. Juliana told me, "Perfection is living into my life-activating force." *Yes*, I thought. *That's it.*

Being perfect isn't about being flawless. Being perfect is about becom-ing as much of myself as I possibly can and sharing her with the world. To be perfect, I must learn how to tap into what makes me feel alive and grateful and content as often as possible. Being perfect, according to Juliana's definition, is the same way I think about being full of my-self.

When I make an awkward joke, I can giggle at myself and, in doing so, show myself some compassion. When I stumble over my words, I can be grateful that I have a voice and not make it mean anything at all except that I stumbled. In doing so, I share all of me with the world and so many people see an example of who and what they can be. That's being full of myself. That's perfection.

Bragging

I have found that most women are scared to brag. They either can't think of nice things to say about themselves or they feel like they need permission to brag. It's "unacceptable" to show so much self-love.

The art of bragging is to talk well about yourself. Becoming skilled at bragging will increase your confidence, and it will be easier for you to embrace being full of yourself.

Bragging rewires your brain to focus more on what you like and love about yourself rather than what you don't. It's not about being braggadocious, too big for your britches, or playing small. It's about honoring who you are and knowing that you're worthy of claiming the space to talk about yourself. I even invite clients, with a bit of guidance, to brag about what isn't working in an attempt to normalize failure and diminish shame.

Here are some examples of bragging:

I brag that I have a great smile.

I brag that I love the shape of my body.

I brag that I love the work I do.

I brag that I don't know what my next career move will be.

I brag that I am writing this book.

I brag that I am struggling with anxiety.

I brag that I am remembering to enjoy the process of writing this book.

Now, it's your turn. Look at yourself in the mirror and brag five times using this sentence:

I brag that _____.

I find that when most women start to brag, they like the way it sounds and feels in spite of the persistent discomfort. They innately want more. For some women, it is excruciating trying to think of five good things to say about themselves. What a wonderful barometer of how much more full of yourself you can become. I also feel empathy for the courage it takes to start to think differently about yourself.

What's also glorious about hearing a woman brag is that the people listening to her light up. I know that I feel better about myself when another woman brags because I'm bearing witness to her greatness. *Thanks for being a beautiful example of what I want more of. You're breathing life into me.*

It's for that reason that bragging is so much bigger than us. When you brag, you give permission to another woman to do the same, and, trust me, she needs to know that she can. I have seen clients take the skill of bragging back to their families and offices. Bragging around the dinner table with their kids. Bragging during work meetings and seeing a shift in culture. Bragging about their partner instead of focusing on what isn't working and feeling the relationship thrive.

Go forth and brag about yourself and others. Remember: we all deserve to talk well about ourselves.

Bragging gets easier with practice. Get started at:

mooresoulsessions.com/workbook

Birthing

I gave birth to my son Charles Austin Moore on March 1, 2016, just outside of Philadelphia. He was born at 4:30 p.m., and I was born 32 years earlier at 4:29 p.m. on an entirely different day and month. There are close to 1,400 minutes in a day, and that one-minute difference feels important to me.

When Austin was handed to me, I didn't fall madly, deeply in love.

One of the first things I asked, with anxiety rising up in me, was, "Does he have all his fingers and toes?" I felt relieved and grateful that childbirth was over and that Austin looked healthy and normal. And yet … I immediately felt infringed upon that I now had to breastfeed even though it was my choice to do so. *My body has grown this human for 10 months, pushed for eight hours, and now you want it to keep giving? What is happening?*

I wasn't fawning over my baby. I was learning how to be a mother to this person I was now carrying in the outside world. We were getting to know each other. My love grew steadily and intensely. Six years in, it is still growing.

I'm sharing this story because I don't hear it enough, or ever, and because it's a great example of a fantasy we are sold. That *hold your child for the first time, and the heavens open* kind of fantasy wasn't my reality. And, because two opposing thoughts can be true, I embraced motherhood seemingly well. Preston and I found a routine, and we worked really well together to juggle our professional and personal needs.

I want women to hear a hundred different stories from moms about holding their child for the first time. It sets us free from our discomfort when it's different from the myths and fantasies that pervade motherhood. I feel solid and content sharing and understanding my experience. I wish the same for others. Your truth matters.

Shoot Me

Four or five months after Austin was born, the three of us went into downtown Philly, walked along the docks, and enjoyed a summer's day out. Short skirts, low-cut tops, boobs, shoulders, legs … I remember seeing lots of skin, and I felt resentful toward these women.

I still felt pudgy and soft after giving birth, and I was uncomfortable that Preston was seeing so much skin. I was jealous of what I thought Preston was thinking. Did you catch that? I had *no idea* what he was thinking. I was too embarrassed and too afraid to ask because I didn't want to look weak. I associated jealousy with weakness, which I am still unlearning.

While I was feeling irritated, I also enjoyed our time together. As we were heading home, I remember driving up a very steep hill in our neighborhood, about to turn onto our street. Within what seemed like an instant, my whole mind and body went numb. All of a sudden, I had an image in my mind of shooting myself. What came next was the scariest part of all: I felt relieved at the thought.

The next thing I remember is huddling myself under my hanging clothes in our closet. It was like I needed to hide and to feel protected. I cried. In that spot, I felt safe to cry. I didn't want to move. Preston found me sometime later, and I told him what was happening. I don't remember much about that exchange except I felt heard, which feels comforting to recall.

I called my midwife shortly thereafter and made an appointment for the same day or the next. I was open about my experience, hiding nothing, and she said that I was most likely experiencing postpartum depression. Those words sounded surreal because I felt as though I was doing great. The truth is, I was. Both things can be true. I'll write it for myself now. Mental health does not discriminate.

I was offered a fast-track appointment to see a therapist and/or a prescription for medication. I decided I wanted to talk to the therapist before trying the medication. With yet another quick turnaround, I was on the phone with a therapist describing my experience. She concurred with the postpartum depression diagnosis and felt that my thought was an isolated incident. I felt relieved. Almost as soon as the thought of shooting myself had come, it disappeared again, as if it had never happened. She asked me to keep a journal of my thoughts to track my progress and make sure nothing scary came up again. I went on my way with no further appointments or medication.

It was scary and a passing blip. Phew. I liked the fact that as quickly as the thought came, it disappeared. It didn't upend my narrative and fantasy of who I was in this new role as a mother. Or so I thought.

The Pump Up Session

The Pump Up Session is dear to my heart. It's an interactive coaching experience and mini-retreat designed to get women out of their heads and into their bodies. I created it after years of leading retreats and public speaking. To this day it still moves me and is often the reset that I crave.

At the beginning of 2020, right before the world as we knew it changed, I was hosting an in-person women's coaching circle that lasted several weeks. Sitting in one of those beautiful circles with 15 other women, lights dimmed, candles glowing, smiles all around, I asked the ladies, "I'm thinking of hosting this event that's like a workout class set to great music, only it's a life coaching class. We would dance and yell and breathe and journal and do other things that I'm not sure about yet. Would you come? Do you like the idea?" A few of the ladies eagerly said yes, which was all the energy I needed to keep my idea alive.

Four months later, I shared my very first Pump Up Session with an audience of fewer than 10 people on Instagram Live. I was nervous as heck. *Would anyone like it? What am I even doing? I'm not a workout instructor. Would the music come through? Would I transition smoothly from dancing to journaling? Would I be able to teach and cue the music in the right spot?* There was only one way to find out. Talk about vulnerability.

I was sharing something that was completely mine. I loved the idea of using music, which moves me so much, to set the pace for a spiritual workout. I liked the idea of being active—dancing, punching and kicking, using our voices, and breathing—to coach our way through our fears and desires. Intuitively, I was drawn to the idea of engaging my body in my healing process, although I wasn't describing it that way at the time.

At some point, I described the class as a pump up session, and thus the name was born. Not too long thereafter I found—or refound, I'm not sure which—the song "Pump It Up" by Endor which became the title track of the sessions. This connection didn't feel like a revelation. It felt like I was onto something, and I was excited.

Over time, the Pump Up Session has stayed true to the initial concept I envisaged when it first came to me, and it has also evolved. All the main components remain: dancing, breathing exercises, meditation, intimate sharing, and journaling. We've done silent sessions in which nobody talks. We've had many sessions guided by a great playlist. Sometimes we play "Pump It Up," and sometimes we don't. It's all about creating a unique vibe that fits that particular experience and group.

One of my favorite pieces of feedback that I still hold dear is how much a woman loved the different pacing. We go from being still and quiet to dancing to an upbeat song. From intimate sharing to shaking. I realized I had unintentionally stumbled onto something important. The pacing was an important piece of the transformation puzzle. Well, I'll be darned. I couldn't have come up with that if I had tried.

I decided to turn the Pump Up Session into a program called the Full of Herself Community and host it on Zoom so I could create a space of connection between myself and other women around the world. There's no intimacy on Instagram Live. A group of wonderful ladies (my OGs) and I have been fine-tuning the experience for over a year, and I'm clear that we have something special on our hands. Our members tell us things like:

This session reminded me that I matter.

I feel anything is possible after attending one of these sessions.

Wow, that was uncomfortable in a way that stretched me.

I needed this time just for me.

This was spiritual surgery.

I feel lighter and clearer.

In addition to Pump Up Sessions, we host guest teachers in the community who are experts in different embodiment practices, from hypnotherapy to theta healing[14] to burlesque dancing to breathwork. I want to expose women to different healing modalities beyond talking.

We also host mini-coaching sessions in a group setting every month so the women have a space to dig deeper into their own lives. Group coaching is powerful because we see ourselves through other people's stories in ways we can't when we are stuck in our heads.

Over the years, I have become clear that the power of the Pump Up Session is less about the content and more about how I lead the experience. I like that insight. It feels true. I like how I am evolving with the sessions. I am less rigid than when I began. I used to script a powerful introduction and a powerful ending in order to pack a punch. I know now that the experience *as a whole* packs a punch.

Scripting it was more about me. I wanted it to be perfect. Now, however, I can be in the moment, trust myself, and guide the experience that I am co-creating with other women. It's a beautiful mindset shift

---

[14] Theta healing is a type of meditation that uses the theta brain wave. I highly recommend my friend and theta healing practitioner, Cara Viana. To learn more or take up this practice, visit CaraViana.com.

and representative of how I am maturing.

Today we describe the Pump Up Session as a fully curated mini-retreat where you reset your thoughts, quiet your internal chatter, and walk away feeling lighter, revved up, and focused on what matters. This session is a no-judgment zone that gives you the freedom to express yourself fully.

While the Pump Up Session has been featured in organizations and on stages and has transformed many women's lives, my team and I desire to see her (and the community) spread her wings and have a much greater impact. She already is. I'm doing my best to stay out of her way.

P.S. Austin loves to play "Pump It Up" and dance around the house. The other day I asked him if he thinks I work hard. He said emphatically, "No. All you do is dance and stuff doing your Pump Up Sessions." Kids.

Why Talk Therapy Isn't Enough

One of my favorite quotes is, "Learning doesn't come from experience. It comes from reflecting on the experience." It is most often attributed to John Dewey, although it's unclear if he wrote these words verbatim in any of his texts.

Reflecting on where I've been, how my day went, or how a conversation panned out is pivotal to helping me create what's to come. Reflection is also a pivotal tool in the coaching relationship. If we don't take the time to assess what happened, how we felt about it, and what the experience taught us about ourselves, we rob ourselves of the opportunity to grow and shape a more aligned future.

I have spent most of my life reflecting through talking, whether that's to a therapist, coach, friend, Al-Anon sponsor, my mum, or Preston. I love to talk, and it's one of my most helpful ways to process. It's also the method I rely on the most as a coach.

However, I came to a point in my journey where I sensed that words weren't enough. About two years ago, I noticed that sometimes talking was starting to hurt me. As someone who has a mind that can go a mile a minute, talking can create unnecessary overwhelm and overthinking. I often end up stuck in a loop of thoughts misguidedly believing that if I just talk more I'll find my way out of the problem. I began to realize that the more I talked, the more I became frustrated and lost. I began to think that perhaps the way out had something to do with my body.

Here's why.

I know that my emotions live in the cells of my body—not in my mind. Based on that fact alone, I recognized that if I'm only engaging my mind, I'm limiting so much of my wisdom that is housed elsewhere. My body is my home. My body speaks to me and yells at me and nudges me and comforts me. I wanted to listen to her rather than ignore her. I wanted to know that an ache in my shoulder is just as important as a thought in my mind. That ache is a signal, a pull toward or away from something if I'll only stop disconnecting that ache from my fears and desires, from how I'm living.

In this sense, my mind isn't my best asset. I started doing Reiki and breathwork, which opened up corners of my body that were stuck and stagnant. I felt more refreshed and certain after experiencing these somatic healing modalities that did not require me to speak. I was experiencing firsthand that changing my body's momentum changed my mind's momentum. It was around this time I created the Pump Up Session.

I'm learning that reflection, for me and other women, is best when it's active. Writing, dancing, walking, singing, jumping, breathing, stretching—as we do in the Pump Up Sessions. Talk therapy is significantly more than most people will ever do, so please keep doing it. It is a wonderful and necessary tool. I'm also clear that it can't be my only tool because reflection, for me, is a whole-body experience.

Geographical Change

In the rooms of Al-Anon and Alcoholics Anonymous, I learned early on that a geographical change is not the solution to changing my thinking and my problems. I still take me with me, after all. I do believe a geographical change—when in alignment and not to escape oneself or a circumstance—is a beautiful thing.

In 2018, we decided to take a road trip to Columbus, OH, along with my parents, to go to The Country Living Fair, hosted by *Country Living* magazine. Having grown up in a home dating back to the twelfth century in the South of England, I love antiques and all things home decor. I spent many a day with my mum shopping for great finds at car boot sales (a garage sale in the U.S.), making the six-hour round trip to IKEA, and perusing home and garden magazines for inspiration. I get my taste and desire to cherish my space from my mum. We have so much fun expressing ourselves through color, fabric, and the hunt for new ideas and items that catch our eyes.

The home Preston and I bought in Philadelphia was huge for a first home at 3500 sq ft and so unusual and lovely. Everybody who walked in would literally say, "Wooow." Not just in response to the architecture of the home and the design choices I made, but to the feel of it. I really made it a home and loved every second of the results.

Going to this fair was a bucket list item for me, so we booked a five-day trip to see what goodies I could find to add to my beloved house. We didn't know anything about Columbus. Within about 10 hours of pulling into town, Preston and I said almost at the same moment, "I think I could live here."

We had been driving around town in the morning and returned to the

Airbnb at lunchtime so that Austin could take a nap. He was two at the time. During his nap, we both found separate spots in the house to enjoy some quiet time. Unbeknownst to both of us, we had each spent two hours googling Columbus, its economy, job prospects, and most importantly, did it have a Trader Joe's? It has two!

We spent the next three days exploring Columbus with the thought of, *Could we live here?* on our minds. After probing and prodding Columbus to see if it would be a good fit, we didn't find anything we didn't like. We loved everything about it.

We drove home to Philly, and that Sunday evening, Preston and I decided to go for a walk in our neighborhood, leaving Austin with my parents. We wanted some quiet time to talk things through. As we walked the streets of our Philly neighborhood, which we knew intimately, not one person made eye contact with us, not even people we knew. Now, you have to imagine, due to the city's history, how narrow the streets are and how close the front porches are to the sidewalk. Very close! After five days of midwestern hospitality coursing through our happy brains, Preston announced, "Fuck this place. We're moving to Columbus."

My parents were in the process of emigrating to the U.S., and we had all envisaged home as Philly. Thankfully, they liked Columbus as much as we did and were ready to pivot. I can't emphasize how many times they have modeled "going for it." It's such a wonderful gift.

We put our house on the market to rent out that week and moved to Columbus three months later—three days before Christmas 2018. I think every day we have lived here we have said, "This place keeps getting better." It's very entrepreneurial, it has a vibrant arts scene, and the shopping is good, too. We're not a major city like Chicago, and with just over two million people in the greater metropolitan area, the city is big enough to have plenty to do and small enough to run into people we know.

The people—that's what sold us. Everyone was so happy to meet us and help us. After eight-plus years on the East Coast, I didn't fully realize how much the gruff culture had gotten to me. When we first moved to Philly, I was excited because the culture felt more akin to England than Texas. I found Texas to be a little fake, and the tell-you-how-it-is East Coast felt more honest and familiar to me. In Philly, my experience was that there's a hardness to life and so people keep to themselves. And so that's what we were used to.

Shortly after moving, Preston and I went to Katalina's (a well-known Columbus spot) for brunch, and when Preston asked for extra salsa, our waitress was so accommodating. Our jaws literally fell open. We had become so accustomed back in Philly to getting extra salsa with a big dose of irritation or inconvenience. The contrast between the two cities surprised us both. Today, it is lovely to know that I had outgrown a culture that felt familiar almost a decade earlier—evidence of my growth and evolution. When that waitress at Katalina's gave us the extra salsa with such enthusiasm, I didn't realize how much I craved "nice."

In Columbus, a good rule of thumb when driving is a mile a minute. At home in Philly, our Trader Joe's was five miles away, yet it took 20 minutes to get there. To this day, almost four years later, we still delight in the fact that, in Columbus, five miles means five minutes. And when it doesn't, and five miles is 10 minutes, we smile. Perspective is everything.

In comparing the two cities, we tell a story that goes something like this:

> In Columbus, I back out of my driveway, in my Suburban, onto a nice, wide, tree-lined street. I drive calmly and easily down the road, and I merge effortlessly onto the highway. Fifteen miles takes 15 minutes, and I pull into my destination where there's free parking, and someone says, "Hey ma'am, come on inside. I'm glad you're here." There's very little stress.

In Philly, seven miles takes 30 minutes. I stop and start and brake and accelerate, trying to weave through the traffic. I get honked at and cussed at along the way while trying to avoid potholes. I hit some potholes and pray that I haven't bent my tire rim. I pay $20 to park in a lot or garage that is not convenient all while timing this journey to very specific hours of the day so I can get where I'm going in a "reasonable" amount of time. It's stressful, to say the least.

All joking aside, we met some great people in Philly, and the city was good to us, but the midwestern charm won us over. We realized how much we were grinding it out every day, and we didn't want that anymore. We wanted to have genuine conversations with strangers that lasted more than a minute. We wanted extra salsa with a smile. I wanted to let go of my armor. I didn't know that then. Columbus would usher me home to myself.

In short, Columbus feels easy. The city is very clean and has a wholesome feel. It has The Ohio State University smack bang in the middle of town, which is very familiar to Preston's hometown of College Station, home to Texas A&M University. In fact, he grew up on a street that sits off the main drag, just a mile or so from campus. We now live on a street that sits off the main drag in Columbus, just five miles from campus in a very similar neighborhood to his growing up. Preston laughs and says, "I think I'm so different, and yet here I am recreating what feels familiar." I find comfort, not disappointment, in that statement because there's something nice about coming home to one's roots.

This geographical change has been one of the best decisions in my life and my favorite move by far. It is evidence that when I work on myself, a geographical change can be a great solution to my ever-evolving wants and needs. I love you, Columbus.

Big Thinking

I attended a coaching seminar early in my coaching journey with the lovely Mastin Kipp. In that room, I stood up and shared that I had a goal to make a million dollars. It was a big, exciting goal that felt like second nature to say, except I was saying it from a broken place. To be honest, I didn't know what I was saying. I was painfully unaware of the strategy required to reach that goal. My business expectations were completely out of whack.

This experience seemed like big thinking when actually it was more about fear. Fear of who I wasn't and who I needed to be in order to be "successful." I've learned that my big ideas can be code for big fear. They can also be code for fantastical thinking. I thought it was my job to run with all of my ideas. I didn't yet know how to harness my big thinking. I have since learned that I can't try to jump to step T when I'm at step B.

I always thought that becoming a successful and well known coach like Marie Forleo sounded dreamy. If I made a million dollars, then I'd be somebody, then I'd feel worthy. Entrepreneurship has reflected back to me all the ways in which I don't feel worthy. Like parenthood and my marriage, entrepreneurship has magnified what already existed within me.

My big thinking told me anything was possible. I no longer believe that. Instead, I believe I can have a dream and put in the work to become more of the person who can hold that dream without having to chase it down. *Easy does it, Sarah. Hang back and see how it plays out.*

Superpowers

For a long time, I have known that my energy is my superpower. More and more I'm coming to the understanding that when you see me shine and you think, *I want what she's having*, what you're really seeing is God's light shining through me. Meaning, I'm walking the path that's meant for me. I'm living with my fists open rather than clenched. I'm not trying to force outcomes to be rich, happy, thin, or worthy. I'm doing what I would call God's work.

I didn't grow up knowing what my superpowers were. I never even thought about my superpowers. Could you imagine if there was a class in school where everyone got to discover what made them special? Where we go around the room and talk about the great qualities we see in each other. Where we make a list of the moments and experiences that light us up and that make us feel alive. What becomes possible for each of us when we instill that kind of thinking?

I had a coaching session with a friend of mine, Cara Viana, a few years ago and she asked me to list my superpowers. It was a refreshing and energizing session. I got to explore a new question and discover what makes me great. It's a list I often think about because it's a road map to live my life my way. My superpowers reinforce *What do I think?*, and *What do I think?* reinforces my superpowers. My superpowers are my strengths and playing to them is my best shot at success.

Here is the list I made with Cara.

- I have a smile that lights up a room.

- I'm courageous (often willing to be the first).

- I make people feel safe and create a special connection.

- I'm sensitive and intuitive.

- I "turn on" when the camera turns on.

- I dream big, bold ideas.

- I delight in and feel a connection to music.

- I savor human beings.

- I'm adventurous.

I haven't reviewed this list as a whole in a while. I am thrilled to say that I am currently using every single one to my advantage. Let's run through them.

I Have a Smile That Lights Up a Room

I am aware that my smile and my energy are more important than the words I use. I recently was hired to do a Pump Up Session for a real estate business in Houston. I was unsure about the experience leading up to it because the room was a mixture of men and women. I designed the Pump Up Session for women, which is the audience I feel most comfortable with. I have worried in the past that men won't relate to it. That I'll ask them to dance, and they'll think, *This is pointless, I'm not dancing.* While I'm scared about what they will think, I'm more scared of what that assumption says about me.

The day before this gig, still unsure, I decided that my energy about the Pump Up Session mattered more than the content. I knew that if I believed it could make a difference in their lives, that would be the factor that would make the experience most potent for them and for me. Whether or not they liked the dancing was none of my business. It also meant nothing about me. That Pump Up Session was a real success. Everyone participated fully, and the owner told me that he was shocked at what we were able to do in an hour.

Regardless of how they felt, though, I knew I was successful because I came with conviction in my offering. In doing so, I practiced what I preach: *What do I think?* I focused on bringing my smile and my energy and my excitement to the session. And I thought I did fucking fantastic. I've learned to smile as an antidote to judging myself. That physical gesture instantly brings a feeling of compassion toward myself and the situation, and I soften.

When I say that my superpower is having a smile that lights up a room, I'm clear that my energy and belief in who I am is the quality that creates the most impact in my life. At that same Oprah event I mentioned earlier, I heard Liz Gilbert say that being on Oprah's stage was not a place to openly share her fear. Liz explained that we know uncertainty and fear intimately. She decided that what we, the audience, needed instead was an example of a woman standing in her power and coming from a place of strength. I liked that perspective and that part of her message has always stuck with me.

Trusting my smile and energy reminds me that my presence alone has the power to move people and is a secret ingredient I leverage. It helps to take the pressure off myself and for that, I'm very grateful.

I'm Courageous (Often Willing to Be the First)

I was the first girl in my school to leave when the bullying ramped up. After that, 11 other girls left within the space of a year.

I was the first to leave a high-ticket mastermind I joined that was no longer in alignment, and several others left after I did.

I was the first to say I wanted to go to South America, not Spain, for my year abroad.

I had the courage to quit my research assistantship during my master's—forfeiting the cost of my tuition in the process—and write for The Eagle.

I was courageous enough to leave the UK and start a life in the U.S. with two suitcases and $100 to my name.

I'm often the first to question something in a group setting if it doesn't sound quite right. I'm comfortable paving the way, and I try to remember that when I think I'm not.

I Make People Feel Safe and Create a Special Connection

As a coach, I am very talented at listening to what you're saying and synthesizing the information you share. These two in combination make people feel seen and heard in a way most people aren't able to. When we're in the midst of a struggle, we tend to feel as though we're swirling. My clients often feel that way, and I certainly do as well when I don't know what to do next.

My clients share a lot of details about their goals and struggles and their innermost thoughts. They are trying to understand the dots and how to connect them. Sometimes the dots work together and sometimes they don't. The women I work with have chosen coaching because there is a gap in the dots, and they are looking for the tools to close that gap and become more effective. Without that gap, there is no need for coaching.

Often a client will end her sharing by saying, "I know that was a lot," or, "Sorry, that was a bit of a ramble." Firstly, I remind her she doesn't need to apologize for expressing herself. Secondly, I emphasize that this is the precise space to share and explore these intricacies. I love hearing all the details because it helps me to build a picture of who this special woman is. I'm very talented at tracking the more subtle dots and seeing how they fit together.

The first thing I always do is thank them for sharing in such a vulnerable way. Do you know how powerful it is for my client to hear thank you, especially when she's already worried that she has rambled on? I don't say thank you to make her feel better. That would be codependent. I'm saying thank you to model that it's safe for her to take up space. When I say thank you, I mean it. I mean it with every inch of my being because it's the privilege of a lifetime to hear the inner workings of someone's mind and experiences.

The next thing I do is take the five to 10 minutes worth of details they shared and distill them into a few sentences. I'll say something like: "Based on what you said, you're worried about A, you want B, getting B would make you feel C, A affects your ability to get B, and because of D that happened last year, you're ready to make a change. Did I hear you correctly, and what did I miss?"

My client is often shocked, in a beautiful way.

My ability to listen to detailed, complex information and quickly synthesize it down to the most important points to identify the gap and how we can fill it builds an incredible amount of trust quickly. My client is relieved that someone understands and can make sense of her needs. I identify the dots as the story evolves, combining them to make a complete picture in my head.

Once we understand the picture as it is now, we can start to build a new picture for the future. That excites me. That excites my client too. My focus on the details—such as children's names, vacations, feelings about a moment in time, what happened with that previous manager seven years ago, etc.—helps to build trust and make my client feel safe, special, and heard. That's why my coaching gets to the heart of the matter quickly.

I'm Sensitive and Intuitive

I think sensitive is a wonderful and positive word that is so often used pejoratively. To be a person that feels and senses my way through life is one of my greatest joys. I continue to learn to trust this superpower and not let other people's judgments of sensitivity throw me off course.

I am also deeply intuitive. I often know what someone is about to say before they say it. I sense in my body if I am on course or off course with my thoughts and actions. I'm often asking myself, *Does this feel right?* While I can't rely solely on my feelings because they are temperamental, I do look to them often.

I "Turn On" When the Camera Turns On

It's true I have a natural affinity for the camera. I have always loved having my picture taken and being the center of attention. I've met a lot of people over the years, and I have noticed that many feel uncomfortable turning the camera on themselves and making a video. They think they don't have anything to say that's interesting.

I struggle with that same uncertainty. I'm also keenly aware that it's important to put myself out there, particularly when it comes to my business. What I have to say could be interesting to someone and irrelevant to someone else. I could make 10 videos that flop, and then something about that 11th video catches someone's attention. We all need to hear different messages at different moments. That's why volume and consistency always win.

I'm grateful that I love the camera and the camera loves me. Back when I worked for the lingerie company, I was interviewed live on the local news. Mid-segment, the newscaster handed me the microphone as she picked up merchandise to show the audience. I instantly started talking about the details of each item and more about the ethos of our company. For me, that felt like the natural thing to do.

After the segment was over, the newscaster said to me something along the lines of, "Hardly anyone starts talking when I hand them the mic. Most people freeze up. You're a natural." That last sentence might be my addition. Either way, I was chuffed to bits. It's amazing the power of a few true words. That was a 12-second interaction, and it has helped to stoke my belief in myself ever since.

After my first speaking gig as a coach, I vulnerably revealed to the host that it was my first time speaking. She could not believe it because I was able to "turn on" in a way the moment commanded using my smile and energy.

The best kind of turn-on comes from an intimate relationship with self. In other words, "turning on" starts with me. When I feel great about myself, the camera captures my big, beautiful magnetic energy. In that sense, the camera is my friend, not my crutch, and is a fun experience that further amplifies my turn-on.

Even in moments when I was younger and uncomfortable in my skin, I've always had a voice. I've always dreamed big. I dream of being on TV and radio one day. Preston often says, "Why would you want to be on TV where there are so many restrictions on what you can say? You already have your own TV channel online. Use it." He's right, and both things can be true. I still want to be on TV and radio. It's a feeling that lives inside of me, and I want to try it out. I'm not attached to how or where I'm on either medium. I want to be able to say that I tried them.

I was born to be in front of people and to create experiences and environments in which people can thrive. I believe that my voice was made to be heard by more people. In the meantime, I'll keep doing my work to become the person who is ready for these opportunities when they come ... because they're coming.

I Dream Big, Bold Ideas

Ask Preston about this. There have been many a day when this superpower has driven him mad. We were once talking about money and how we were struggling to pay the bills, and I said, "Well, we could sell up and move to Bali. It's a lot cheaper there." I was completely serious. He looked at me like I wanted to jump off the moon.

When I was living in Seville, Spain, on my last night before flying back to the UK, I decided to take every last penny I had and book a room at the Hotel Alfonso XIII, a luxury hotel that is one of my favorites I have ever stayed in.

Deciding to buy a lake house in a town that I had been in for precisely 24 hours was big, bold, and courageous (more on that story later).

Writing this book was a big, bold dream that I had envisioned for over 20 years. The part that was particularly bold, and that I am particularly proud of, is that I didn't get caught up in learning how to write a book or wondering if I was good enough. I trusted that my best way forward was to start writing. I knew I didn't need to get ahead of myself worrying about editing and publishing and that those next steps would reveal themselves in good time.

Dreaming big, bold ideas is akin to *going for it.*

I Delight in and Feel a Connection to Music

I adore music. It moves my soul. Wherever I am—whether in a particular moment or location or phase of life—is all the better for music. I like to dance. I have hips that can move. I love to sing. I intentionally sing to relieve stress and change my emotional state. From all my years playing the piano, I am well-versed in singing a section over and over until I get it right, and that repetition brings me peace and joy.

I couldn't imagine a world without music. I'm proud of how I've woven music into my work through the Pump Up Session, and I'm clear that music is the critical element. As a side note, when I die, I'd love to come back as a singer with the talent of Whitney Houston but with a healthy sense of self.

I Savor Human Beings

What's funny about this superpower is that I can take or leave other humans. I recently went to a conference, and I consciously chose to dance alone rather than with my friends because I felt less awkward and more free. After that experience, I started describing myself as an extroverted loner. It rings so true. I am both introverted and extroverted, as we all are.

I definitely need time to recover after being with people, which is a hallmark of an introvert. I also wildly enjoy hearing people's stories and marveling at what they have created and cheering them on, when I'm in the mood. If I'm not in the mood and I'm feeling insecure, I'm likely to write you off and not give you a chance. If I'm in the mood and I think you're interesting, I'll savor your whole being.

I'm Adventurous

Each of my superpowers is infused with adventure. I'm quite charming by nature and that adventure lives in my spirit. In my approach to a conversation, in my choice of words (for example, do I want to be provocative?), in my decision to dance in the checkout line. An adventure isn't something I go on in the mountains, although that could be true, too. Adventure is who I am. *I* am the adventure.

The Mastermind

In 2017, I joined a mastermind that I hoped would skyrocket my business. I paid over $40,000—that I didn't have—to be a part of it. I felt so sure that I was supposed to be in that group, like it was a calling from God. I didn't feel a desperate urge to act which is usually a sign that I am pushing my will. Instead, I felt a calm certainty.

I was at a point in my career where I wanted more. I wanted to be more visible, to earn more money, to reach a higher level of success. Until that point, I had tried everything I knew to do and felt stuck. I had plateaued at making $25,000 a year, my events were the same size and not getting bigger, my email list had remained at 250 people for years, and I wanted more. I felt I was capable of more.

Joining this mastermind represented an up-leveling—a decision to be around people who were playing a bigger game than me, whose thinking I could be exposed to, whose systems I could replicate, and whose inside knowledge I could use to fill in the gaps. I still feel so proud when I think about myself standing at the front of the event that was the precursor to the mastermind. With a huge smile on my face, I told the rest of the room that I was ready to invest in myself with this decision. I loved putting my intention out into the world for others to witness.

More than anything, I was betting on myself. I was reaching higher. I felt so aligned and poised to grow in ways I had only dreamed about. I also want to mention that Austin was a year old, and I had aced the first year of motherhood. I felt powerful and sure, and my primal energy was very much, *Mother I am, hear me roar.*

In the first six months of that mastermind, I made precisely $0. I was about $14,000 in debt from the $3,000+ monthly installment I was paying. I didn't know it at the time, but my mental health was starting to wane. I was becoming increasingly frustrated that the decision, which had felt so aligned, was starting to feel off.

The mastermind included retreats throughout the year which meant chances to meet in person, collaborate, grow, and fine-tune ourselves and our businesses. One retreat was in Nashville. I had purchased the top-tier mastermind option which meant that a handful of us got an extra day at the retreat. I was excited about the hands-on attention and for that extra time to think and be.

I left Nashville feeling bewildered and worked up. I was not impressed with the extra day. I wasn't clear how it benefited me. I didn't feel seen or supported in my ideas and the feedback from peers felt misaligned. I felt further away from my own inner knowing than ever before. To boot, I wasn't recouping any of the money I was spending. I felt the pressure that had been mounting for months.

When I signed up, I felt so sure that I would quite easily cover the cost of the mastermind, at a minimum, based on the alignment I felt with the leader and my experience that I could leverage. Yet here I was feeling helpless, sad, uncertain, and disillusioned. In reality, having never made more than $25,000 in my business in a 12-month period, I was asking myself to make a 66 percent increase in sales. Even with that increase, I would have made zero profit based on the cost of the mastermind. In reality, I needed to make $65,000 just to break even. My strength for big-picture thinking limited me in being able to think strategically. My mind typically just says, *Go for it*, without fully considering the finer details.

Halfway through the year-long mastermind, I decided to put on a signature event that I called Soul Sessions: The Extravaganza. I felt I had a lot of traction in my local community, so I boldly rented out a theater that had a capacity of 250 people, The Venice Island Performing Arts

Theater in Manayunk, PA.

I thought now was the time to step up, take a calculated risk, and stop playing small. I invited a pretty well-known speaker in the coaching world to speak at the event. She said yes. That was another wonderful sign. It's also important for me to mention that I was a member of a number of networking groups where I was very visible and at which I had spoken several times and built some credibility.

No word of a lie, three weeks before the event I had sold nine tickets. I was in tears. I didn't even want to lead an event, let alone one called The Extravaganza. I wanted to cancel the whole thing and give up. I was embarrassed and felt like a failure. After gathering myself together, realizing it was not too late to get my deposit back from the theater so I didn't lose more precious pennies, I pivoted and rented out a local yoga studio where I ended up having The Extravaganza for about 14 women. I remember feeling frazzled walking into that event and grateful that there were some women who said yes.

This event was a precursor to selling a mastermind of my own. It's a common sales strategy, the very same one that got me into the mastermind I was a part of. It's not salesy in a sleazy way, as long as you approach it with integrity. The theory is that the speaker delivers so much value and you feel the energy in the room so intensely that you can't help but want to continue learning and sign up for an extended, more intimate experience.

When I look back, my primary goal in hosting The Extravaganza was to increase my revenue. I wanted to up my impact and visibility. I wanted to prove that I could bring more women into a room. It wasn't about anyone but me. I'm very sure that changing women's lives was a byproduct. That's the ingredient I was missing from the start. I had become so focused on being seen as a success that I had forgotten what the work was really about.

At the end of The Extravaganza, nobody bought the mastermind. It's not that shocking based on what I just shared. To be honest, I was relieved.

Shortly after The Extravaganza, I was advised by my networking friend, David, that I couldn't continue with my mastermind commitment because it was bleeding my family dry. I will always be so grateful for David's mentorship. He was right. The monthly payment and the experience itself were starting to create a lot of stress because of the misalignment that was surfacing. I left, and many others followed. I subsequently found out that the mastermind leader also felt out of alignment with his offering.

I learned an important lesson from that decision. I learned from David that when I disregard logic and go for it, I put enormous pressure on the situation and myself to produce a certain outcome. In my mind, it *has* to produce. It *has* to work because there's no room for anything else. Burning the bridges to reality can sometimes be beautiful, and other times disastrous. Never again will I sign up for something I can't afford. The big dreamer in me isn't always so practical, yet I have evolved significantly thanks to this cornerstone experience.

Writing this, I can sense my fists clenching, my body tightening, and my feet digging in. Have you ever thought about how too much of a good thing can apply to strengths? An underbelly to strengths that most people aren't talking about is that we use them to excess. We often know one or two strengths intimately and come to rely on them too heavily which creates an imbalance and limits our potential.

Ideally, we want a balanced ratio of strengths so we can function at optimal capacity. At that time, I didn't know that I could over-index on a strength and have it work against me. I didn't know that my big thinking, which I always admired about myself, was creating so much tension and exhaustion. I didn't know I could turn the dial up and down on my big thinking strength. Shit, I didn't even know there was a dial. I just lived life going for it. And, in doing so, I stressed the hell out of my nervous system.

I want to be able to afford investments so I can let them be what they need to be. I want to give them room to breathe, to evolve, so that a single outcome isn't the marker of success. Listen closely. I could have made $0 and said it was a shit experience. Where would that have gotten me? Resentful at the leader, my peers, and myself? Blaming coaching, saying it's a messed-up industry? Blaming myself for making a mistake? With a commitment to self-awareness, I can always find a growth opportunity if I want to.

I constantly remind myself that nothing is happening to me. It's happening *for* me. That is a fundamental belief that steers my life. I signed up for that mastermind thinking it was going to be a great next step. And it was. It just wasn't the step I thought it was going to be. That was a hard, humble pill to swallow.

The mastermind was never about getting to the next level financially. It was about getting to the next level in my thinking. It was about unlearning some of my unworthiness patterns. It was about reshaping my relationship with money. I'm so grateful that I was able to see and grasp this opportunity.

From this experience and others, I am clear that I am my own compass. Nobody is ever going to know what is best for me and my work better than I am. I have learned to trust my instincts first and to seek help from a place of curiosity, not desperation. Sometimes it gets confusing in my head because never would I have said that I felt desperate when I joined the mastermind. Maybe I wasn't. It was simply the next best step in my journey. I do know that never again do I desire to believe that the answer lies outside of myself.

Friendship: My Side, Your Side

A friend told me, much later on, that during the launch of The Extravaganza in 2017, she had called for support, and I didn't call her back. According to her, I then called her a couple of weeks later to ask her about buying a ticket, and I didn't mention the fact she had called. She felt hurt by that. She felt that I didn't make time for her. My actions turned her off. She was resentful for months.

While I don't remember the specifics of these calls, I believe that my actions hurt her. I could see the hurt on her face. Her experience rings true to me. I was focused on the fact that I wasn't going to sell enough tickets. I was overly focused on myself and trying to control the outcome, thinking that the more I worried the more control I had. My side is that I was selfish and missed out on an opportunity to be a good friend.

In turn, my friend didn't voice her concern at the time. I noticed there was a distance between us in those months and trusted her to talk to me if she needed to. I told her that she could have told me what was bugging her, that doing so was a very valid option, and that I probably would have acknowledged my part. She agreed. And at the same time, I acknowledge that she didn't need to tell me quicker than she did because it can often take time to process our own thoughts and feelings.

I trust that there was an opportunity for her in the waiting. I know I've certainly waited longer than seems necessary *many* times because there was something I was afraid of or trying to unwind, dissect, or come to terms with. There is no right or wrong amount of time to reach out and talk to someone. There is no right or wrong amount of time to reach out and make amends. At the end of the day, reaching out is better than not, even if it's 40 years down the line.

When I'm upset with someone, it can be easier for me to blame the other person than sit with my discomfort. It's important to remember that I often have a part, too. I try to clean up my side of the street as quickly as possible, meaning that I do my work and then take the correlating action to be ok with myself and my part.

Never did I set out to cause my friend pain. It's an important example of how I can cause harm without knowing it, especially when I feel less than and small. I inadvertently make the other person small, too. By cleaning up my side of the street, I minimize the amount of energy I expend on things that aren't working well. I want to put my precious energy toward something productive—a dream, joy, meaning, purpose.

Whether we sit with something for days, weeks, months, or even years, whether we say something or we don't, no matter what we do, we're walking our path, and we have to trust that.

Meaning

I attended "The Forum," a personal development training course through Landmark in early 2017. It was an incredible program, although very masculine in its execution. Imagine 12-hour days with very little moving around in a boring, gray conference room. That part I don't miss or wish to repeat. The profound message, however, that came like a raging bullet at the end of the weekend was life-changing.

The message was: life has no meaning. At first, I was a little taken aback. I thought, *Of course, my life has meaning. If my life doesn't have meaning, what's the point of my life?*

I took a moment to let the words sink in, and I understood the message. I softened. I started to smile. I had spent the past 36 hours of my life trying to get myself and others to understand the great meaning in the pains and triumphs of my life; to try and unravel the meaning that had knotted me into a bunch over and over again. I understood that my efforts were futile, and I felt relieved. Others became paralyzed by the message and got stuck defending their position—which just goes to show how easily we can resist doing our work.

By nature, we are meaning-making machines. That's part of our survival encoding. It's innately in us to make meaning out of everything in order to make sense of our world. Why not develop the skill of having that meaning work in our favor rather than shooting ourselves in the foot? I quite literally disable myself all the time, limping in place, unable to move much at all because of the negative meaning I have assigned to a particular moment. It's bonkers.

Let's imagine Preston says something that hurts my feelings. He says, "You're flaky with your work. You're always changing your mind." He has actually said this to me. I made this to mean that I'm not consistent, that I'm not good at business, and that I'm failing. This interpretation would be an example of shooting myself in the foot. Let's be clear: *I* gave that meaning to his words. Best case scenario, his words have no meaning. They're words, and *his* words to boot. I can run them through my filter and decide if they're true using the question, *What do I think?*

Or, I can decide that his words show concern for my work which means he cares. I could also decide to apply his words and see if there are any valid points so I can become more effective. Gosh, to have that response immediately feels like the work of a lifetime! Oh, to be that kind to myself and him. And yet, it's possible. That's why my self-awareness practices are *vital*. I have to take care of my spirit so that I can be poised to choose these routes over being a victim.

That day at "The Forum," I could taste the freedom in life having no meaning. This concept is a tool that works well for me. It doesn't mean I'm not special, that my life doesn't have a purpose, that my relationships aren't a gift from God. Not at all. What it does mean is that I learn how to navigate the limitations of my brain. Making meaning out of everything as a way to have certainty and outrun vulnerability does not make for a great life. It's paralyzing and debilitating.

Still, I have much to learn because when Preston says something I don't like, my first thought isn't, *It doesn't matter what you're saying because life has no meaning anyway.* It's more like, *How dare you criticize me.* Ha! I'll keep doing my work.

Three Things

At any moment in life, we are doing one of three things:

1. Making a decision

2. Experiencing an outcome

3. Pivoting

Our ability to move through these three phases relatively quickly is directly correlated to our overall level of contentment and success. Most of us get stuck in one phase for longer than we need to be, and we wonder why we aren't where we *want* to be.

Let's say you desire more connection with your partner. It's something that you have been thinking about for a while, the desire feels true and real, and it's growing roots. You could say to your partner, "I'd love to feel more connected. Would you be open to talking about ways in which we might do that?" You've made the decision, and you've asked for what you want. Now you're about to experience an outcome.

Let's say you felt nervous about asking your partner. Maybe you're worried they'd look at you funny or blow you off. There could be any number of reasons and stories for why you'd stay stuck here. Any time we're stuck, it's a signal to dig in and do more of our work so we don't blame the other person. Blame will only keep you more stuck. Some people stay stuck here for years telling themselves they have a partner that won't put the relationship first when the greater truth is … they never even asked.

When you ask for more connection, you likely feel exposed because the question is vulnerable. Remember, the definition of vulnerability is uncertainty, risk, and emotional exposure. The exposure you feel upon asking is an outcome.

You might hate the feeling so much that you decide it's not safe for you to ask such intimate questions. Instead, you stuff your feelings deep inside. That could be especially true if your partner dismisses your request. Your partner might also be very supportive and want more connection, in which case you move forward together. Either way, you're experiencing an outcome and making meaning out of it that works for you or against you.

Based on what you learn from the outcome, you pivot. If you're practicing self-awareness consistently, it will be easier for you to pivot. If your partner turns you down, you might be less willing to take it personally. In that case, you feel your feelings (perhaps disappointment and anger), and you decide that perhaps your partner is stressed, and it wasn't a good time to ask. You'll try again later, maybe in a different way. Your thinking is the pivot.

Perhaps your partner turning you down represents a long list of letdowns, and you start to get honest about whether this is the right relationship. Perhaps you need counseling alone or together to understand what the future holds. These are pivots because you're not getting stuck in the outcome. You're moving forward remembering that you're responsible for yourself.

As Brené says, "When we pretend we can avoid vulnerability, we engage in behaviors that are often inconsistent with who we want to be." [15] In other words, you're left with a huge gap between what you want and your ability to get it. Anytime there is a gap in skill, knowledge, or belief, coaching is a great option.

---

[15] Brown, *Daring Greatly*, 45.

Working with a coach in a moment like this can be pivotal. The conversation isn't going to revolve around your partner. It's going to be about you. It will be gentle and powerful and confidence-building. A coach will help you name your feelings and surface any limiting thoughts and behaviors that are getting in the way of being consistent with who you want to be.

Paying attention to these three phases can help you identify where you are in any given situation, from tiny to monumental. They are a guide to help you take a step forward and get unstuck. Ask yourself, "What decision can I make?" or "Do I need to pivot?" The outcome is a landing point in between.

Career Developments

Within a week or two of The Extravaganza finishing and having left the mastermind, I decided to stop coaching completely. I kept saying, "I have done everything I know how to do, and it's not working. I even paid to work alongside the pros, and I'm still no further ahead." Looking back, everything was working except my worthiness. I felt broken.

If I could have understood the impact I was having and that what I thought I wanted wasn't what I really wanted, that would have been fantastic. But that was not meant to be my journey at the time. I thought I needed *more* to feel worthy—more money, more followers, bigger events, more important people asking me to speak, more praise. I didn't yet know that worthiness comes from accepting what already exists.

I felt absolute relief stepping away from coaching. I was physically, emotionally, and spiritually spent. At the time, someone said to me, "Don't quit right before it gets good." What I heard her say was, *Don't run away*. Quitting couldn't have felt like a more foreign word. My poor, sweet soul knew she had taken a hit and needed room to breathe. I didn't feel as though I was running away. I felt as though I was running *to*—running to pain to break me down, running to myself to begin again, running to God, running to peace, running to humility, running to a long, deep breath.

I spent 18 months working a few jobs and researching different career opportunities. I listened to all the whispers and explored them. I looked into getting a Ph.D. and talked to friends in higher education. I let myself try on the idea for size and ultimately realized it didn't fit. I submitted an application to work in higher education as a coach, and it wasn't to be. I researched coaching jobs in corporations, asking myself if I could still coach without the pressure of having my own business. I turned over lots of stones and felt satisfied by the exploration. That still didn't answer the question of what came next for me.

In order to make some money, my accountant offered me a job as his assistant during tax season. I said yes. I loved that job. It was an absolute gift. I got a steady paycheck, I had somewhere to go every day, and it was simple. It gave me a real sense of purpose. After tax season was over, I reached out to a friend who owned a real estate company in Houston about a remote job. Preston and I had dabbled in real estate and had the desire to invest in the market.

My friend offered me a job identifying deals on the market. We were both thrilled about the combination of his growing business and my coaching expertise. I found a deal that was exactly the kind of deal my friend, who was an expert, would have jumped on. We all got excited. My skills seemed promising. With the little bit of real estate experience I had, I wondered if I was staring my dream in the face.

It quickly ramped down from there. I was regularly frustrated with a colleague who wasn't providing me with enough direction. I was desperate to fit in, desperate to get it right, desperate to be a part of the team since I was working remotely (before being remote was a thing), and desperate to understand the system. I remember crying a lot and thinking, *What I'm feeling doesn't match the reality of the situation.*

In reality, my struggles had nothing to do with anybody else and all to do with my longing to find myself and my place. It was an intense, emotional time. After a few months of working in this company, my friend was gracious enough to let me come to the conclusion that this was not the best fit for me, and I left. I am still so grateful for that time.

A couple of days later, we took the trip to Columbus, and you know what came of that. A new adventure to a city we wanted to be in. On our first day of that initial visit, I applied for a corporate coaching job, via an online listing, at a Columbus-based company that seemed right up my alley. It felt like a sign. The job was coaching the call center team. During the initial interview, the owner very quickly said to me, "I think you would get bored with this work." Instead of listening, I barreled through his comment, asserting my interest and fit for the position. Deep down, I knew he was right, and I wanted it so badly.

Then, our discussion ramped up from call center coach to coach for the entire company. The proposed salary had tripled, and we were putting together a framework for this new position. One of the executives said that this job was all but mine. I was thrilled. I couldn't believe that I was moving to a new city and finally carving out the type of job I had always envisioned. A few days later, I received a simple and nondescript email from HR saying they would not be moving forward with anything. I was crushed.

The truth is that I was not ready for that kind of role nor was I built for the original role. I was ahead of myself and ignoring myself all at the same time. I was still learning to listen to my intuition and to understand what was right for me, not just what seemed right. I am so grateful for the CEO's intuition and experience. I am also grateful they pulled the plug. That season of my life was a whirlwind.

During one Columbus visit to set up our new life, we were staying in an Airbnb that was modern and sleek … and void of a soul. There were no bedside tables, no lamps, no coffee table, no decorations at all. It was so depressing, and I felt so sad. That apartment looked how I felt: increasingly empty. The house we wanted to rent had fallen through, and Preston was interviewing in Cincinnati, two hours away, so I was spending the day alone with Austin. I felt burdened by motherhood, not necessarily as a whole, but by the many hours I was facing alone. I was so down, so sad, so unseen, so alone in the world, so unable to voice my needs. I felt lost.

I ended up booking a massage upon Preston's return that I was grateful for and that still wasn't enough to cure the ills of my soul. As I came out of the massage, I remember feeling distressed that if a massage couldn't help me, what could? What was I going to do now? I had pegged a massage as the ultimate luxury. I didn't know that the far greater luxury was serenity from the inside out. In hindsight, the move was masking so much of the depression I didn't know I had.

I spent that fall finding a tenant for our home in Philly, packing, finding a new home, making multiple trips to Columbus to lock everything down, finding a new preschool, saying goodbye to friends, selling items we no longer needed or that wouldn't fit in our new townhome, and visiting Preston's family in Texas for 10 days.

It was a lot of hard work and provided a different focus from the ongoing search for where to land with my career. I was excited because we were the ones *doing something*. This was a moment for that part of me who likes to be the best. I liked the attention, the dazzle of being the ones who are so "brave." I also loved how we came to the decision to move. It felt so easy, so natural, and that made me marvel.

We moved two days before Christmas and began to settle in. We couldn't have been happier. As we were settling into our new city, I accepted a job selling insurance. I was so pumped about the opportunity. I thought about the decision very carefully and concluded that it was an avenue I wanted to explore. I liked that it was entrepreneurial in nature, that there was a team of wonderful people I could be accountable to, and that I could use my coaching skills to help me succeed. I could see myself rising through the ranks, building a team, and, over time, transforming from insurance agent to coach.

This job was a great fit in so many ways, except I didn't like selling insurance. *No matter*, I thought. That was a small detail in the overall plan. The company and the culture were fantastic. To this day, I still admire the work they do. Similarly to my real estate job, I kept finding that my emotions didn't match the reality of the situation. I lasted three months in that job until everything went sideways.

I was coming out of a time when everything felt hard and forced with my coaching business. Clearly, I continued to unlearn some of the same lessons while searching for my next career move. Maybe the answer could have been less outward searching and more inward instead. I needed to grapple with life and face these lessons head-on to understand what it all meant.

I find the twists and turns of life to be exhilarating and extremely painful. I look back at this season of my life and marvel at my curiosity and my courage. I kept putting one foot in front of the other, ever willing to see what was around the next corner. I'm also laughing thinking about how I thought the insurance part of the insurance job was a mere detail. Ha! I live, and I learn, and I grow.

Parenting

As Austin grew, I often felt full of rage. To this day, it still rears its head, although I am learning how to work with it and have more discipline around it. It particularly came to the forefront when Austin was a little over a year old, which happened to be the same time that I joined the mastermind.

I was making an impact on women's lives, I had clients I loved, I had people buying tickets to events I was dreaming up and creating, I was raising my beautiful boy and learning how to be a mother, and I was understanding partnership with Preston as a parent. I smile thinking about how good it all was. I just didn't know it.

Looking back, my mental health was declining. I was reacting, struggling, hopeful, up and down, joyful, and trying to get through the day. Since I wasn't sitting in a closet crying and unable to function or having more extreme thoughts of shooting myself, I had no reason to be alarmed. I had no idea what depression was. Now it seems totally reasonable to think that if I'm yelling and screaming because I'm a little frustrated, there is reason for alarm.

As my sense of purpose was dwindling, I started to become increasingly frustrated with Austin. I yanked him around when he wouldn't brush his teeth. I screamed and yelled at the top of my voice when he wriggled around as I tried hopelessly to change his diaper. I once hit Austin across the face when he was having a complete meltdown. Who was *really* the one having a meltdown? I swore I would never be a parent that hits. It pains me to write this. As someone who puts on the armor of perfectionism when I feel uncertain, it's hard to admit that I'm flawed. What will you think of me?

At home, it seemed like everything changed overnight with Austin. In Philly, we had stair gates, he used a high chair, he had a toddler bed, he wore pull-ups, he went to bed easily, and we made him pack lunches for preschool. In Columbus, we had no stair gates, he upgraded to a big boy bed, he didn't need a high chair, he was completely dry, bedtime became a nightmare, and there were no lunches to pack because his new school provided them. While everything about our move and parenting to that point had been relatively smooth, so much changed with Austin so quickly.

In Philly, our house had a lot of stairs and since we slept on two different levels, we locked him in his room for safety. Austin was two at the time, and we thought it was a genius idea. It gave us peace of mind to know he wasn't going to fall or try to climb anything. We tried the same maneuver in Columbus even though our new home didn't have the same safety concerns, and it totally backfired.

At the time, because he was fighting bedtime with everything he had, it felt like a natural decision to keep locking him in his room. We would leave him for a few minutes and then check on him. I didn't account for the fact that he was getting older and was more aware of his surroundings. In hindsight, he was in a new room, in a new house, and it was scary for him.

In his old bedroom in Philly, he didn't know any different. We could see him on the monitor. He would tooter around his bedroom playing, babbling, snuggling, reading, and now and then he'd try the door handle. *Oh, it doesn't work. No big deal.* He'd go right back to what he was doing. He rarely got out of bed, and if he did it was 10 minutes before he went to sleep and 10 minutes after he woke up, at most. He was completely content in his safe space, and we were content that he wasn't going to fall down the stairs and off a 12-foot balcony.

As bedtime became increasingly fraught, something that lasted hours wore on my every nerve. I am not proud to say that I yelled and screamed. I pounded my fists into Austin's headboard, right above his head, in total frustration and rage. I wanted so desperately to enjoy my evening, for it not to consume my whole being. I was at a point where I dreaded bedtime even when it wasn't my night, where I was thinking about it before it even began. Preston and I watched parenting videos, read books, and tried new methods. Nothing seemed to work. This change in circumstance came as a total shock to the system. My sweet boy who was easy to put to bed and had slept 12 hours a night since he was three weeks old just would not go to sleep.

I feel uncomfortable to this day that our sweet, lovely neighbors had to hear me scream. I wanted to know what they thought of me, so I could manage how they saw me. Especially when one of them babysat Austin and knew our family. There's another part of me that doesn't want to know how they felt. It was like I was one version of Sarah in the world and a different version at home; a secret Sarah that only my neighbors and my family knew about.

For so long, my anger and frustration toward my son were a source of shame. Having shared my story—writing really is cathartic I feel more compassion for myself than ever. In retrospect, I believe Austin was responding both to his environment and my emotional precariousness. I felt overly emotional about "small" things. I often felt disrespected by Preston. Sometimes I was embarrassed by the way he spoke to me, and I couldn't stand the finger-pointing cycle we were in.

During a trip to Texas in the fall, before we moved to Columbus, we were at Preston's uncle's house for a family party. In the middle of the party, I found myself at the point of sobbing. I had no idea why. I went to the study, locked the door, and cried a good, hard cry. I remember sitting in that room, looking at framed newspaper clippings and publishing awards and family photos … and feeling so lost and alone. Preston didn't seem interested in meeting my emotional needs.

One of his favorite lines and beliefs, which comes from Alcoholics

Anonymous, is, "That's not about me. That's about you. That's yours to figure out." While I wholeheartedly believe in self-responsibility, I often felt so pushed away and hurt. I would become enraged. I would swallow my feelings, causing them to burst out sideways. While I cared about the parenting struggles we were having, my temper was short and my fuse was close to burning out.

Of course, I wish I had had the tools to spare my child and myself that reality. I wasn't supposed to, though, because it was part of the experience of growing, of having my child teach me how to better emotionally regulate. I also learned that Austin wasn't doing this *to* me. He had needs that I didn't know how to meet. I believe our children can be our best teachers if we will let them. I have worried about the emotional damage I may have caused my little boy. I have also forgiven myself. I am clear that I am doing Austin a greater disservice if I continue to hold onto that pain and shame because I rob him of the joy of today. He needs me to be present, and I can't do that if I'm stuck in the past.

Why do we not have schools that teach us how to parent other people and ourselves? How to have healthy relationships? How to understand money's role in our lives, and how to manage it and welcome it? Why do we not have schools that teach us about intimacy and sexuality and the wildly complicated and fascinating nature of our bodies? That teach us how to navigate hard conversations and take care of our emotional health? In my opinion, these are the things that matter most.

In the meantime, I'll keep educating myself on how to parent this lovely little boy of mine, and most of all, myself.

Shoot Me Continued

I was doing some Al-Anon step work with a friend who lived in Houston, and while getting into the nitty gritty of my feelings and behaviors, I said to her, "Do you ever feel so angry that you want to kill yourself?" She responded, "No, never." I was shocked. "Never?" I replied. "Wow. I feel that way quite often." Soon after, I asked Preston the same question. He also said no. I genuinely couldn't believe what I was hearing.

My experience of wanting to die felt, to me, like a normal response to the amount of rage and sadness that lived inside of me. The two went hand in hand. I mean, if I'm that angry, of course I want to die. At the time, it felt like the most natural correlation in the world. Now, with more tools in my toolbox, it doesn't make sense like it did then.

I now know that wanting to die was a tranquilizer. It was a way of coping with my feelings. Nobody is supposed to be that pent up, that low, so we need a pressure-relief valve. And what better way to make the pain stop than to die? It's the ultimate cure. Not a great cure, but a cure nonetheless. Suicidal thinking was my remedy for life feeling too much, and those thoughts started to ramp up. I was having them multiple times a day. I would be driving down the road, and I'd imagine swerving off it, or plowing into the car in front of me, or swerving into oncoming traffic. When I crossed train tracks, I would imagine the train killing me. When Preston was rude to me, I'd imagine shooting myself. My mind became stuck in this thought loop.

I never had a plan to kill myself. When you have a plan, you are suicidal. When you have thoughts about dying without a plan, those are considered suicidal thoughts, also known as suicidal ideation (SI) in the clinical world. I never knew there was a difference. Sometimes, I make that distinction for people when I tell my story. I would like to think it's to educate people, which is important. In reality, it's mostly because I feel that SI sounds less serious, and that way I can manage what people think of me.

One morning, I was supposed to be driving about two hours north for a meeting about the insurance job I had just started. At home alone, I stood in the kitchen, in my dressing gown, waiting for the kettle to boil, getting ready for my day. As I was waiting, I was thinking about how lonely I would feel making this drive. I was in a new state, Ohio, and I was headed to an area I didn't know. The sadness filled me up. And then I envisaged driving myself off the road.

That thought felt more dangerous than any other thought I'd had in my life. I didn't necessarily feel I was *going* to drive off the road. For the first time, I did feel as though I was too unsafe to drive. With the kettle still boiling and my nervous system on absolute overload, I started to cry, which quickly turned into a heaving sob. I sank down and crouched into the fetal position. I couldn't have stopped crying if I wanted to. I howled from a deep, guttural place inside me.

I called Preston and described what was happening. He suggested I call a friend to get a different perspective and then go to the meeting. I don't think he knew how to help me. He didn't grasp the depth of my distress, nor did I completely. He thought a "get on with it" strategy might help—which did, sometimes. I know that my life can get better when I get back on the horse. I did as Preston suggested and called a friend who told me to have a shower and then go out for a walk. After the shower, I was still considering whether or not to go to the meeting. I tend to do that; I make something important that is unimportant. But, then again, my commitments matter.

I went for a walk, came home, and continued to sob. I felt shaky, weak, and overwrought—like I couldn't keep going the way I was going. I kept coming back to this new feeling that I didn't feel safe being out in the world alone. I made a call to another friend, Di, who, when I described what I was feeling, said that this was nothing to mess around with. Di said she didn't know the best thing to do so she was going to call the suicide hotline—which just sounded strange and unfamiliar to my ears—to get some advice. She made me promise to wait for her to call back and to pick up the phone. I promised.

Di called me back and said that the hotline recommended that I call. It still didn't sound real. As I dialed the hotline number and heard the phone ring, I felt like this was unnecessary and that I would be fine. Even though I had these suicidal thoughts and I felt low, I rationalized that I could find my way through it. Now that I wasn't sobbing, it wasn't that bad. I mean everyone has a moment in their kitchen where they drop to their knees, feeling desperate, lonely, and like they aren't safe to be alone … right?

I described everything that had happened that morning and the kind male voice at the hotline recommended I go for a psychiatric evaluation. Those words didn't fit my narrative, so I had a hard time digesting them. *Me? Are you sure?* I could have hung up, done nothing, and soldiered on. That's a frightening thought. I'm so thankful that I was willing to listen to my friend and to the hotline operator. In 12-step rooms, we say, "When the pain is great enough we become willing to make a change." I guess my pain was great enough to listen and follow through.

I described to Di that Preston thought I was ok enough to go to my meeting and that it would probably help me if I did. While I was on the hotline call, she called him and reiterated what she had told me earlier; this was serious and nothing to mess around with.

Here's a miracle, among many, in all of this. After our move to Columbus, Preston made a career change. He had spent years working in flooring and had recently been hired at a local mental health and addiction hospital. Preston made a call, and two hours later, we were driving to the hospital for my psychiatric evaluation. It was our ninth wedding anniversary. We giggled to normalize the uncomfortable feeling we both felt on that day of all days. That's the beauty of building a life together and sharing the most intimate and vulnerable moments.

I thought this evaluation would be quite clinical. It turned out to be what I would best describe as an informal two-hour chat that was gentle and loving. Preston sat in the room with me to provide a different perspective. When you're in distress, it can help to have a loved one not in crisis present to provide some different context. At first, the nurse suggested admitting me to the hospital for five days. Just like when I was on the hotline, I thought, *Me?* And then I said, "You think I need to stay in the hospital? Will I be with crazy people? Will I be safe?" My stomach turned at the thought. She saw the look on my face, and we talked a little more.

She left the room, and when she came back, she suggested that intensive outpatient treatment (IOP) three days a week would be the best option. I am not sure what changed her mind. I didn't want to know because I was grateful for a plan that didn't scare the heck out of me. My nervous system was already overloaded. It was becoming clearer and clearer, second by second, that this was more serious than I had imagined.

I started treatment very soon thereafter, which was a surreal experience. I was nervous the first day I made the 18-minute drive from home to the hospital. Three days a week for three hours a day, I was in a room with 12 other people who were learning how to develop better coping mechanisms. I put my insurance job on hold. I had a candid conversation with my mentor about what had been happening, and I haven't backed down since when it comes to being honest about my mental health struggles.

I remember feeling some embarrassment and discomfort about what clients would think when I went back to coaching. Should I tell them?

Was I being authentic if I didn't? How could someone with such a recent mental health struggle possibly help them? For years, I had heard Preston tell stories about his experiences in an IOP program to get clean from drugs and alcohol. I took comfort in the fact that I didn't have those problems. I had always been the Al-Anon, glad that I didn't have to drink and drug to escape my feelings. And yet, here I was in the same place, with years of Al-Anon and coaching under my belt and in desperate need of help. I worried about how that looked.

I'm smiling as I write this because I realize that this experience was an important moment in my development of a growth mindset. At the time, I was worried. *Shouldn't I know better? Am I a good coach if I don't know how to help myself?* I want to give that girl a kiss and a hug, thinking she was immune to struggle. It's similar to sober alcoholics who hide their past drinking and recovery from their employers. We are all so afraid of what others will think of us in our most human moments that we label ourselves as unacceptable and unwanted.

As the first session of treatment began, led by a brilliant master's level counselor who I took to immediately, I was faced with some shock and discomfort that I was in a room not just with people struggling with their mental health but also addiction. There were people who had used the night before when they said they wouldn't, people who had just gotten out of jail, people whose families had been killed. My first thoughts were, *They don't separate us out? Am I safe with people like you? Eww, jail? If I'm with you, what does that say about me?*

As I listened, I quickly settled in because I identified with what these people shared. I listened to everything the counselor had to say, I asked lots of questions, and I started to see myself (and the others in the group) in a new light. I learned that the difference between me and them is how we choose to handle our thoughts and feelings. They used drugs and alcohol to numb, and I used suicidal thoughts, as well as control, achievement, and codependence. We weren't that different after all.

In fact, on the inside, we were struggling with exactly the same issues. I heard every word my peers said, and I scribbled away in a little notebook that I still reference to this day. I'm so grateful I didn't let the presenting circumstances of others, which seemed so different from my own, prevent me from getting the message.

Every day at the beginning of class, I had to rate my anxiety, depression, and suicidal thinking on a scale of 1-10. That exercise made everything all the more real. I had to fill out a form that was a plan of action for when I had suicidal thoughts. On that form, I was asked if I had a gun in the house. *Oh my God, this is too much. I'm not going to kill myself. I'm fine.* We did have a gun, though. To keep me safe, the counselor and I agreed that Preston's job was to make sure there was a safety catch on it and that it was hidden. I still don't know what that safety catch looks like. I hadn't thought about the gun until the question was asked. I was grateful I didn't know where it was because from then on, sometimes when I had a suicidal thought, I would picture using the gun.

As I sat in a chair in rehab, just as Preston had years before, I was overcome with emotion to think our paths were crossing in a way I couldn't have imagined, and that felt like a gift from God. I was able to understand Preston's experience in a way I couldn't have before. My life was on the line, too. Even though he is the addict and I am the Al-Anon, we are still suffering from the same disease of addiction.

I'd spent my whole life feeling either superior to or less than others. Judging others is a distraction from the judgments I feel toward myself. During the five weeks of treatment, my whole being surrendered. I gave up the fight, the struggle, the insanity. My body got a chance to breathe. I loved everyone in that treatment room. I had to listen. I wanted to listen. I was ready.

I am beyond thankful to say that my suicidal thoughts began to subside. As the sessions went on, I realized—in what felt like a single moment that was as clear as day—that I was supposed to be coaching. It was such an easy, easy whisper to hear that I trusted it completely. I didn't have to second guess or overthink it. The words that kept bubbling up in me were, "Sarah, stop running from the thing you love." My dear friend Cara said to me one day, "I've never seen you more in your power. You're not running. You never ran, and you never left coaching. This was coaching all along." Those words rang so true.

It took an immense amount of courage for me to say, "I have done everything I know how to do in this coaching business, and it's not working." As I've already shared with you, it's not that it wasn't working. It was. The trouble was in my unrealistic expectations of how to grow a business and what success means to me.

Taking time away from my business ultimately brought me closer to myself. The space allowed me to completely fall apart and breathe. I didn't yet know how to chase my dream and breathe at the same time. I became very clear very quickly that I had been strangling my dream. I was so tied to a particular vision of how it was supposed to look that it didn't have any room to breathe either.

During that time away, I often heard myself saying, "I think I'm still supposed to coach. I just need to be open to it looking differently." The fact that I was willing to try out ideas that felt like reimagined versions of what coaching could be was liberating. Even though I knew I was returning to coaching, I didn't rush. I didn't have to. I was too busy focusing on my own wholeness—which is exactly where I needed to be.

The day I got out of treatment, I found out that I was hired as a contractor for a coaching company I loved. I had applied for the job eight months earlier while I was still living in Philadelphia. At that moment, I knew how marvelous life can be when I get out of the way.

How Are You?

When someone asks how I am, I strive to give an honest answer. I'd encourage you to do the same. We don't need to be afraid of each other. We can practice trusting ourselves and others with the truth.

Our stories are what connect us. I have realized that when someone asks me, "How are you?" there is an intimacy in sharing something that happened in my day. I might respond, "I'm great. I got the good news that our offer was accepted for the house we want to buy." Or, "I'm feeling grateful because I started working with a new client who is so insightful. I'm so grateful I get to work with this person."

If you're not fine, practice saying you're not fine. Say, "I'm tired," or, "I'm struggling today. I had a hard conversation with my husband," or, "I'm feeling a bit out of sorts this morning because I didn't spend time meditating and journaling." Here's the most important part to remember about sharing: Don't give the other person every last detail. You might think you're being vulnerable by spilling your guts. You're not. As I once heard Brené say, "Oversharing is the opposite of vulnerability." It's a lack of boundaries. A little information, however, can go a long way to building relationships.

I even enjoy sharing about my depression and suicidal thinking, in moments that feel safe, both with people I'm close to and sometimes with total strangers. Since I know how to share with boundaries, I have built lovely moments of connection with lots of people. The things I learn about people are extraordinary. That's what vulnerability does. When we're vulnerable, it gives others permission to be vulnerable in return.

Now, let me say that sometimes I don't answer honestly or completely because I don't want to. I may say, "Great," and keep it moving. I love having that choice, and it's perfectly acceptable to me. Sometimes it's healthier for me to say less and/or keep the focus on someone else.

To this day, I still enjoy people's reactions when I answer such a simple question with more detail than they were expecting. We ask, "How are you?" as if there is a social agreement we all signed that says, "I'm not really asking you to hear an answer. I'm asking you because I'm supposed to." No thanks. I'm not interested in that agreement. I want to share the human moments afforded by that question.

If it feels as if my answer is too much for someone, or they don't know what to do with such an unexpected reply, I do a quick *What do I think?* check-in. If I feel comfortable with what I shared, I remember that what they may or may not think is none of my business. After all, I have no idea what they're thinking. If I feel uncomfortable with my reply, I do my best to be aware of my discomfort and address it as quickly as possible. My rule of thumb is, if something doesn't sit right with me about my words and actions, I say something. For example, "I've been thinking about what I just said and it's not what I really meant. Here's what I was trying to say ..." I might also say, "Was what I just shared ok for you?" Or, "Did I hurt your feelings?" If I don't circle back in the moment, I do in the future, whenever possible, because I want to feel clear and complete.

Crucial to the interaction is to ask, "How are you?" in return—and mean it. I do my very best to look someone in the eye and have energy in my voice as I ask that question. I'm not asking to ask. I'm asking to understand. Many of us are asked how we are doing, and we answer thoughtlessly, then immediately rush into saying what we need. Answering thoughtfully and then repaying the courtesy of asking the same with curiosity is a beautifully simple way to help people feel seen and heard.

While I'm a proponent of neutral thinking, as I mentioned earlier, there's still a time and a place for honesty, even if it might sound more negative. If I'm tired and I share that sentiment with someone, you might say it's not a great example of being neutral, and I would agree. I also know that as someone who often wants to look good to other people, it can be important for me to admit when I'm not doing well. Not to create a pity party or to make myself feel worse, but to practice voicing my emotions so I can acknowledge and accept my truth. Only once I do that can I start to heal.

Only you can determine your motive. Start by asking yourself, "How am I?" so you can begin to develop an understanding and language around your inner state. You now have a foundation from which you can create more connection with yourself and others as you navigate the vulnerable act of conversation.

Journal Prompts

Here are the journal prompts we have collectively used and shared over the last two years inside the Pump Up Sessions in the Full of Herself Community. I love exploring myself through these questions. They provoke insight and, oftentimes, relief as I hear other women sharing similar struggles. Together we lay down our burdens and find hope through our own and each other's honesty and healing. Feel free to mark this page and circle back to this list of questions any time you need a prompt to help you come home to yourself.

- I can embrace my beginner by …

- Greatness means …

- What does humility mean to me?

- What do I desire?

- When I'm not trying to figure it out, I …

- Dancing means _____ to me.

- Speaking up means …

- What makes me feel beautiful?

- My body is trying to tell me …

- I'm being reminded that what's important is …

- God wants me to remember that ...

- The seeds I'm planting are ...

- List 20 things I have accomplished this year.

- Peace means ...

- What am I resisting?

- I foster community by ...

- My life is unmanageable when ...

- When I feel (insert the feeling you'd like to explore), I can ...

- I want to take care of/clear out ...

- My body wants me to know ...

- How did I people-please this week?

- How am I brilliant?

- What does community mean to me?

- How do I play the victim?

- Who am I at my best? At my best I am ...

- What am I unsure about?

- What do I think about (insert any situation I am uncertain about)?

- What would my life look like if I was responsible for what I can be and let go of the rest?

- What worries are on my mind? What can I do right here, right now about that worry?

- What am I most proud of today?

- Who am I pretending to be?

You can find these journal prompts with plenty of space for writing and reflecting at:

mooresoulsessions.com/workbook

Success

Aclose friend of mine, Shelly, has a business that nets seven figures every year. She has low overhead, has built the business from scratch, and has no employees. This setup affords her a great sense of freedom. Shelly is in control, doing something she loves. One day at my house, I told Shelly what a success she is. She replied, "Am I really?" Her response stopped me in my tracks. By most people's standards, Shelly is a success. For her, however, it has felt different.

Let's start by saying that Shelly knows she is successful because of the business she has built and the woman she has become in the process. What she also feels is an uneasiness. A nagging sense that somehow this journey would feel different. That there would be an arrival point where a feeling of fulfillment would set in, and she could finally feel content. That hasn't happened for her.

Shelly told me that she excels at defining success for herself in the short term by naming the next milestone to aim for. Defining success in the macro isn't so easy so she has forced and pushed and hustled to get to the next pitstop on the journey that might satisfy the emotional cravings she has. Shelly didn't understand what it meant to be in alignment as she was scaling this business. She didn't know what it meant to fully trust her intuition. She did what she did best. She got busy doing. In this way, she did not feel successful because she was too busy chasing down her worthiness and didn't know it.

Boy, can I relate. This has been my journey in business for a decade. I automatically ascribed success to Shelly because of all the zeros she has earned. When I think about success, it's still so easy for me to be impressed and allured by money. I had compared myself to her and found myself to be coming up way short in the money department. That's why her words stopped me in my tracks and showed me, once again, my flawed relationship to success.

As a European, I admire the American can-do energy of the land where "anything is possible." After 17 years here, I am unlearning the insidious aspects of consumerism and capitalism and how, little by little, they have affected my sense of self and my decision-making. They are not to blame, although they play a role. Why don't we hear people talk about their debt-to-income ratio, the intimacy in their relationships, the quality of their daily life? These are incredibly important markers of success and sources of true fulfillment and worthiness.

I define success for myself as every moment I'm true to myself. That definition keeps me content, in alignment, and at peace. My body gets the chance, every day, to feel in her bones, that little bit more, what success really is.

I often ask my clients, "What is your definition of success?"

Here are some of their answers:

> Peace.

> What I have is enough.

> Knowing that I am in control of my future.

> Knowing this can have a successful outcome.

> How much fun I'm having.

> Living a life that feels good in all areas as often as possible.

You'll notice that money didn't come up. I have never met a woman who defined success with money at the forefront.

Most people assume they know what success means, and yet they don't know their definition of it. Take the time to think about your own definition of success. Your definition guides your everyday life. It helps you choose in moments when you're unsure and helps to shape you into the person you'll become.

Success defines the path you walk. My success lies in more healing, more alignment, more allowing. If you don't know your definition of success, how can you possibly know where you're headed?

Women

I recently watched comedian Bill Burr's brilliant comedy sketch, "Women Failed the WNBA."[16] His commentary was in the context of equality of the sexes, particularly when it comes to pay in women's versus men's professional basketball, among other sports in the U.S. Women complain about how little WNBA players make, and yet they also don't really support female sports. The money goes where the attention goes. He talks about how the WNBA doesn't sell many tickets, while *The Real Housewives* and *The Kardashians* make millions thanks to their high viewership—from women.

Clinical psychologist Jordan Peterson points out that men are often accused of being aggressive and women are not. He makes the argument that women *are* aggressive, just not physically. They're aggressive when they're tearing down other women because they don't want to see them succeed. How often do we look at things as a zero-sum game? If she's winning, I'm not.

It's interesting what we complain about versus how we cast our votes with the dollars we spend and where we choose to put our attention. More women would rather watch women bitch at and fight with each other than go out and support women being the best in their sport and demonstrating excellence. I know it's much easier and more accessible to turn on the TV than it is to buy a WNBA ticket. Still, I want you to think about that.

Writer and podcaster Glennon Doyle, who is one of my favorite people to follow on social media, posted a video of herself dancing on her boat

---

16 Bill Burr, "Women Failed the WNBA," 2022, Comedy video, 4:34, https://www.youtube.com/watch?v=QY9Gz_IMn_k.

in Florida, singing songs she loves, and feeling on top of the world. That day, she had the highest number of unfollows she's ever had in one day. Glennon concluded that it was hard for people—I'm going to assume mostly women—to see another woman look and feel full of herself.

Questioning our worth is a hallmark characteristic of women in a society dominated by men. We're fighting hard trying to be equal to men. I often wonder if what we really want is to be recognized for our strengths because we are different from men, and there is a need for us to be respected for our unique experiences and perspectives.

These stories are all the proof I need that we women must do our work to stop tearing each other down and start cheering each other on when we thrive. How do you treat other women?

Catcalling

What woman wants to hear catcalls and be whistled at while walking down the street? Not this woman. If a man yelled, "You look hot," or "You look lovely," instead of whistling or hollering at me, I might think, "Wow, you are vulnerable enough to say that. Thanks." I'd like that.

In the absence of an actual compliment, I feel like I'm being drooled on, gawked at, and hassled. It's unpleasant, and I often feel unsafe when it happens. In Argentina, the word for a catcall is *piropo*. If my memory serves me correctly, the men would literally make sucking sounds as I walked by. It was gross.

As I was driving home today, I saw a lady running. She had water bottles around her waist in a special velcro harness, and she looked like one of those serious runners. I admired her because a runner I am not. I think she was checking herself out in a shop window she was going by (at least that's what I do). As I was passing her, I thought to myself, what if I roll down the window and yell, "You look great!"

I saw a TikTok trend recently where two people were driving around, and the driver would yell, "Hey, that color looks amazing on you!" or "Hey, you have a beautiful smile!" to random people on the street while the passenger filmed. At first, you can tell the people think they're going to be harassed. And when they realize they're getting a genuine compliment, their faces completely light up.

What if women start catcalling other women? What if we speak empowering messages to each other that celebrate all aspects of ourselves—sexuality included? What if we reclaim the word "catcall" as a shared "I see you" moment that is conveyed with solidarity and love?

We could hoot and holler and shout things like, "You look hot. I see you working hard. Atta girl. Go get 'em. Keep going." I'm getting excited just thinking about it. I know I'd feel weird at first both giving and receiving these words and then it would leave me feeling giddy— a little like bragging. I'm willing to feel weird if anyone else is on board. Shall we start something new?

Full of Herself Wheel

I love the Full of Herself Wheel, which is inspired by the wheel of life. It is a marvelous tool to assess your life holistically. Too often we make decisions in silos not knowing to ask ourselves how a financial decision, for example, will affect our social and intimate relationships, our health, our personal development, etc. Every decision we make has knock-on effects, sometimes in areas we wouldn't imagine. The Full of Herself Wheel provides a roadmap for thinking about all areas of our lives and how they may be impacting one another.

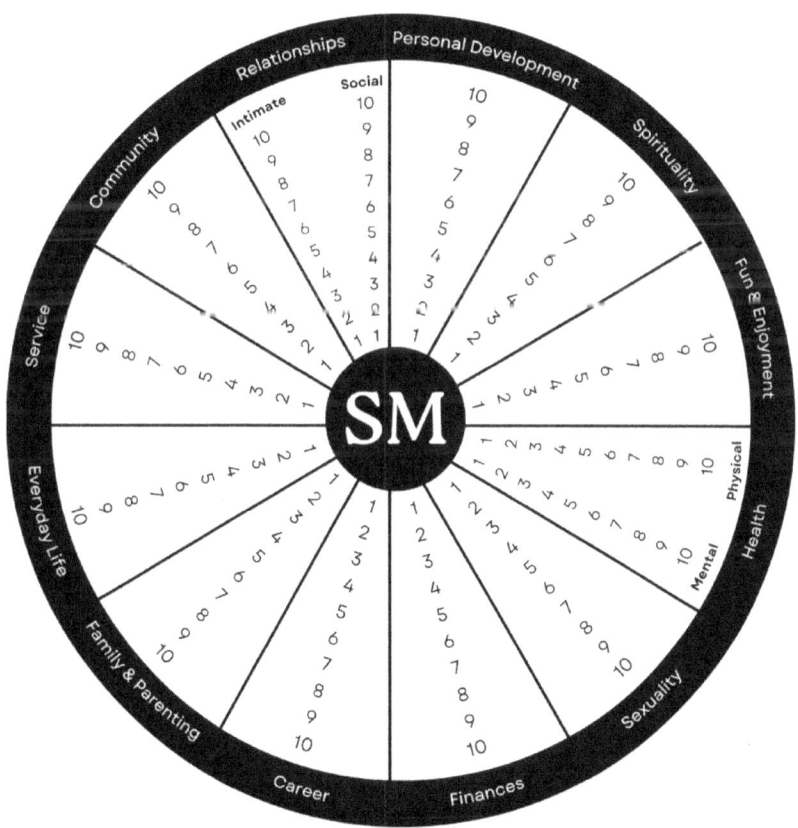

The wheel shows the major areas of our lives in segments. To complete the wheel, choose the number on a scale from 1 to 10—1 being crap and 10 being amazing—that best represents that area of your life at that moment. Don't overthink it, and use your gut. Once you have assigned a number to each segment, join the dots in an act of kinetic transfer to see your wheel. I have never seen a round wheel.

To assess your wheel, ask the following two questions in this order:

What about my wheel surprises me the most?

What area do I want to focus on that could support my growth?

Some of the best leaders I have coached use this tool, even if it's a checklist in their head rather than literally filling out the wheel. They use it to understand what's at the root cause of their struggle. Let's say Maria is worrying about a meeting that was challenging. After sitting down and completing the wheel, she discovers that she scored low on physical and mental health because she hasn't been sleeping well. Maria learns that the presenting issue—in this case, the challenging meeting—is not the culprit after all. The root cause is the lack of sleep which has created irritation and lowered her tolerance for difficulties.

I recommend using the wheel regularly. There are no right or wrong answers, simply information to steer you home to yourself.

Wondering how to apply this to your everyday life? In the accompanying workbook, I have provided some thought-provoking questions to help you understand each segment of this wheel in detail. Get your very own copy at:

mooresoulsessions.com/workbook

Stop Living in the Present

Reposted from mooresoulsessions.com/blog
Stop Living in the Present, December 15, 2021

I know that you're energized by the idea of growth.

You like the idea of living to your potential, and as one client, Nina, put it this morning "opening myself up more to life."

In order to grow, to fully experience the awe and wonder of life, you have to develop self-awareness.

To know what motivates you, what you're afraid of, to take responsibility, to be accountable.

Here's a nugget about how to do that even better.

STOP LIVING IN THE PRESENT.

For most of us, living in the present is a disaster.

These are the words of the father of positive psychology, Martin Seligman. I attended one of his lectures this week, and his words stopped me in my tracks.

Stop living in the present? All I hear about is living in the present.

As I started to ponder this idea, here's why I believe this message adds up.

We're all yearning for agency, which is perhaps the underbelly of personal development.

Agency is described as a belief that I can accomplish good things in the world.

Agency correlates to progress, to heightened well-being in all areas of life.

Lack of agency correlates to stagnation.

In that same lecture, I learned that agency consists of three building blocks.

The first is efficacy: the belief that "I can accomplish a goal now."

The second is optimism: the belief that "I can accomplish this goal in the future."

The third is imagination: the belief that "There are different possibilities, a whole range of scenarios for how I might accomplish my goals. I even have a whole range of goals."

In short, being present-minded is one barrier to optimism and imagination.

To use our imaginations means we have the ability to innovate, we try, we are resilient. We can't be innovative, try and fail, and bounce back solely in the present.

Furthermore, I started thinking about my own life. Knowing that I'm going on holiday to Florida in January is bringing me so much joy. The anticipation is wondrous. There is nothing more wonderful than having something to look forward to, something to aim for. Not to escape life, not to hurry it along, but to enrich what already exists.

COVID has been disastrous for so many of us because that sense of future was removed or shortened.

Living in the present is starting to sound less and less appealing, and unrealistic, for how we are wired.

I'll also add that practices to stay in the present such as meditation and mindfulness are wonderful and necessary prescriptions for anxiety and acceptance.

Living in the present is an incomplete story.

Let's start enjoying the joys of the future, too.

With love,

Sarah x

Garth Brooks

On a regular Friday, Preston and I spontaneously bought tickets for a Garth Brooks concert that same evening in Cincinnati, which is two hours away from Columbus.

I highly recommend being spontaneous. It made me feel as though I was really living.

Garth's show was a masterclass in generosity. My immediate impression was that the show wasn't about him. It was about us and the incredibly talented musicians he plays with—think Grammy winners, talented songwriters in their own right, folks who play 10 instruments. I started to write "his" musicians and quickly corrected that wording. They are their own people, after all.

It was a stadium tour, and we were inside the NFL Bengals stadium. Garth ran around this huge, circular stage, at 60 years old, while continuing to sing, for over two hours. For reference, I jumped around for about 30 seconds and couldn't finish the chorus to his song, *Baton Rouge*. He literally ran his tail off paying homage to every single one of us and, in doing so, created a shared experience.

What really got me was this: at the end of almost every song, Garth looked to the heavens with this look on his face as if he couldn't quite believe that he just got to sing that song and have that exchange with us.

There was no sign of him thinking, *This is my 500th show and I'm gonna get the job done*. For me, he displayed gratitude and humility at the highest level.

Garth's encore was him and his guitar, no band, answering almost every song request and question that somebody held up on a card. From giving out guitar picks and honoring young men and women serving our country to singing his songs again and songs he barely knew, he showed up for the people who showed up for him.

Thank you, Garth. As someone who often takes a stage, even if it's one on Zoom, I will cherish the leadership you provided, and pay that forward. And, here's me thinking I was going for a night of music. Well, that was pretty great, too. That was my first Garth show, and hopefully, it won't be my last.

I subsequently read up on Garth and watched his great documentary on Netflix, *Garth Brooks: The Road I'm On.* I wanted to understand how he was able to pour into people the way he does and not get exhausted and burned out. To my delight and shock, I learned that being on stage is the very thing that energizes him, that feeds his creativity and soul.

I started to think about how I lead. After an event, I need time to recover. Some of that may be the way I'm wired. Some of it might be the way I'm showing up—being too uptight, making it all about me instead of leaving room for an exchange that fills me up. I don't need to be like Garth. That's not the point here. I am energized by his example and how it might shape my leadership, and it leaves me with something to ponder.

Could being on stage leave me feeling alive and wanting more? If it's possible for Garth, it could be possible for me, too.

Generous Assumption

The theory of generous assumption is one of my favorite leadership tenets that I learned from Tony Robbins years ago.

The theory goes like this: When someone says or does something, be generous in your assumption of them. Don't look for the flaws, or the ways they are trying to get you, or what you think they really mean and aren't saying. Take the stance of generosity, meaning that you assume they are doing the best they can, even when it looks ugly.

This theory is one I work hard to remember in my relationship with Preston. It's easier to act like a jerk with the people I love because there is so much comfort and intimacy between us. It's also easier to be more generous with people outside my home because I don't know them intimately, given that I typically spend short amounts of time with them. We all know what it's like to be feared up (the way I like to say afraid) and say something we don't mean. What do we need at that moment? To be reprimanded? Or put in our place? No, what we need most is compassion. It takes generosity on our part to give that to another person, especially when they are acting like an ass.

Assuming generous intent is an act of giving, which requires trust. As a culture, we're a little short on trust these days because we only tend to give something once we get to know someone enough to trust them. What would it be like to trust first? To give generously without needing explicit proof of trust? As Preston once heard in a Tony Robbins coach training program, "Our lives expand in proportion to the generosity of our spirit."

Part of my approach to the theory of generous assumption is to believe what someone is telling me and showing me about themselves. I don't look for hidden meanings. I try to take what they're saying for exactly what it is. People teach us who they are through their words and actions.

If someone is constantly demonstrating that they are unreliable, it's up to me to notice that. I don't want to be bent out of shape because they keep showing up late. I know this about them. I am not surprised because they have been teaching me who they are all along. I can choose to be generous by letting them be late—which is them doing their best even if it's not my best—and not feeling secretly resentful. I can also choose not to.

I have to be self-aware enough to know if I'm measuring people against my standards or enjoying letting them be who they are. If the behavior is more extreme, or it's causing me harm, I can choose to step away from the relationship acknowledging that it's not the best fit for me. In that sense, being generous doesn't mean that I have a lack of boundaries, that I'm being trampled on, or that people are taking advantage of me. Not at all.

By noticing what people are teaching me about themselves, I can leave the drama at the door and generously make the decisions that make sense for me. I'm not holding you hostage or pointing the finger. I have the mindset, *You're great, exactly as you are, and I'll decide to stay or keep on moving.* What a gift. Please remind me, though, of this generosity the next time Preston says something I don't like.

Difficult Conversations

Most days we are faced with moments where we need to communicate something that feels a little edgy, and we lack the skill or the confidence to say it. I once heard Fred Kofman, executive coach and culture and leadership advisor, say in his Conscious Business Coaching program, "There are no difficult conversations. Only conversations we don't know how to have." I still think some conversations are difficult no matter how adept we might be at having them. Difficult might refer to the circumstance as opposed to skill level, which is how I mostly think about it.

We are experts at making up stories that we then interpret as the truth. I can't tell you the number of times a client has said something like, "I think my boss is mad at me because I disagreed with him in the meeting." And I say, "Have you asked him if that's true?" The response is nearly always, "No. And it seems so obvious that I could ask now that you've said it."

Since we're meaning-making machines, creating our own story provides some safety. We know how to live in the story. We're less adept at moving into reality. Mostly because we haven't learned how, or seen it modeled. I spend a lot of time modeling how to approach difficult conversations for my clients.

For the most part, clients present me with three approaches to difficult conversations. One is to tell the other person exactly how they messed up, point your finger, and stand your ground. This is never a recipe for success, even if the other person is being, well, difficult. It creates defensiveness and separation. The second approach is to say nothing and stew quietly. This definitely doesn't work either because the other person lives rent-free in your head.

The third approach is the one I hear the most. It's to share how the experience impacted you, do so in an honest and relatively evolved way, and leave it at that. While better than the other two approaches, this misses vital pieces of connection and belonging because it's not a conversation. In short, it's all about you. It doesn't invite the other person in, nor does it give an opportunity to broaden your perspective.

I want to share Fred Kofman's Difficult Conversation Model, which I learned in his program. The following steps are his words, and the explanations are offered through my lens while doing my best to honor his system. It's one of the best models I have seen, it's the one I share the most with clients, and it provides a framework to help you improve your difficult conversation skills.

Step One: Define a mutually beneficial purpose.

Approaching conversations as collaborations—a moment to come together—is mutually beneficial because people feel united by a shared sense of purpose.

In layman's terms, you might say something like, "I'd like to have a conversation about how we can succeed together." Other options might include:

"I want to have a conversation about how we get on the same page."

"I'd like to chat about what's been going on so we can better understand where we're both coming from."

You're essentially laying the foundation for, "How do we both win?"

Step Two: Express your point of view.

As I illustrated before, this is the only step most of us take when having a difficult conversation, assuming we're already on a path to self-aware-ness. At best, we tend to thoughtfully think about how the event im-pacted us and then share that truth and call it a difficult conversation. This part is important when accompanied by the other four steps.

In layman's terms, share what it was like for you rather than blaming the other person. Practice saying "I" as much as possible. "You did this …" only creates antagonism and pushback. It's much harder for some-one to argue with "I felt …" or, "My experience was …" or, "When this happened, I did …"

If you take one thing away from this model, take this: When you have finished sharing your experience, say, "That was my experience, and now I'd love to hear about yours." Doing so is a great lead-in to step three. You have not finished expressing your point of view until you have asked the other person to share their experience and perspective.

Step Three: Understand their point of view.

As outlined above in Step Two, you can begin by asking, "What's your perspective?" or "How are things for you?"

Understanding someone else's point of view means you listen. You ac-tually seek to understand. You do not interrupt. You don't ask ques-tions. You let them talk. Encourage them. Nod. When the other per-son has finished talking, you may ask clarifying questions, and until then your only job is to zip it and be curious.

Step Four: Negotiate a mutually beneficial strategy.

In a business context, you might be literally negotiating. You might need to lower the price, extend the timeline, add more people, etc. In this case, you are trying to negotiate a deal that works for all involved.

In other cases, when the negotiation is centered on coming together and understanding a path forward, what you're really asking in layman's terms is, "What can we agree on that meets your needs and mine based on everything we have just learned about each other?"

Step Five: Make a commitment to execute.

Making solid commitments to one another is the part we tend to forget and fall short on. A failure to get clear on commitments creates room for resentment. Imagine you're in a work meeting and Susan says that she'll do her best to get the information to you by Tuesday. You hear Tuesday, and when the end of Tuesday comes around and you haven't heard from Susan, you start to feel a little antsy. *Huh, she said she would get back to me by Tuesday. That's annoying. Why haven't I heard from her?*

What we're saying in layman's terms is, "What commitments are we making to one another that we can do differently moving forward?"

At this very moment, as I'm typing this, I'm waiting to hear back from an organization that promised me some information by this afternoon, at the latest. It's important information, and I'm a little on edge because I thought I would have received it by now. I'm reminding myself not to make up stories that aren't true and to be generous in my assumption. I'm also allowed to be frustrated because they haven't done what they said they would do, and I can hold them accountable for that. This situation is also a great reminder that I want to be impeccable with my word. Meaning, when timelines and circumstances change, I communicate them ahead of time. If at all possible, I don't wait until the last minute to keep people in the loop.

When we make commitments, "I'll do my best" isn't an acceptable answer because it creates ambiguity. Neither is, "I'll see what I can do." Both of these statements, in reality, acknowledge an inability to commit, even though they are often said following "yes." There are three clear answers. "Yes," "No," and "I can't commit to 'yes' yet" because one of four things is needed: clarification, conditions, more time, or alternatives. Some examples include:

1. "I need to clarify what you want to include on the agenda to make sure I can run the meeting on your behalf."

2. "This could work for me, on the condition that we increase the budget by $2,000. Is that possible?"

3. "I commit to getting back to you by next Wednesday regarding your idea. I need time to think about it."

4. "I can't commit to sitting down and helping you with all your homework. I can sit down and help you with the first part and, as an alternative, how about you check in with me after you finish the second part?"

In a training that I did with Fred Kofman, he said this:

> "Our effectiveness depends on the integrity with which we exchange requests and promises that allow us to coordinate our actions. The bonds of trust strengthen or weaken our commitments. Do I promise frivolously or default carelessly? If I do, I harm relationships and betray my values. That's why commitment conversations carry huge consequences. There is a correlation between the impeccability of commitments and the effectiveness of individuals and groups."

The root of the word integrity is from the Latin *integrare*, to make whole. When we live with integrity, we are engaging in the act of making ourselves whole. That's why our commitments matter.

While I have centered this example around work, think about how being impeccable with your commitments could improve your family life. Do you consistently promise to load the dishwasher and don't? Do you tell your kids, "Yeah, I'll play," and then find yourself on the couch making excuses? Now they're whining, and you're annoyed. Little by little, our frivolous words erode trust. We owe the people we love the most a firm commitment either way so that maximum thriving can occur.

Let me be clear. It's ok to change your mind, or for something else to come up. In those cases, it's your job to communicate clearly and openly about changing circumstances and needs.

Once you have clear commitments established, it's also very important to get a second yes. This is a check-in moment for all parties, a chance for impeccability to shine through. If Susan says, "I can commit to getting this project done by Thursday," together you will check the following:

1. Both you and Susan understand the request in the same way.

2. Susan has the resources to complete the request successfully (time, skills, budget, etc.).

3. Susan has a plan that accounts for even small things going wrong.

4. Susan will manage the plan by tracking progress and communicating with other parties.

This scenario with Susan is an example of a simple business commitment. If you are using this model because a conversation has gone awry or tempers have flared, you will find yourself making behavioral commitments. Maybe you commit to being more open-minded and not jumping to conclusions. As a result, when you go for the second yes, you can:

1. Confirm that "open-minded and not jumping to conclusions" mean the same to both of you.

2. Talk about what you need to be doing personally for that to be a possibility (perhaps more reflective time in the morning) or what resources you need to be successful in this regard.

3. Decide what you will do if you find yourself getting off track. Might you excuse yourself? Might you have a code word with the other person to help bring you back into the moment? The options are plentiful.

4. Sit down once a month/quarter and use the framework of the Difficult Conversation Model to review your progress.

I have learned a lot from Preston about the impeccability of my commitments. I used to be a person who wouldn't do something if I didn't feel like it. I changed my mind a lot. I love exercising the right to change my mind. It's very important to me and a crucial tool. I also now love being impeccable with my word. I love being the one who shows up. I love being a person people can rely on. I love noticing how many people don't show up and realizing what they're missing out on, what I would have missed out on. I love the relationships that I have built because I have shown up. I love to see what it means to other people that I show up.

Being impeccable with my word has become a satisfying part of my life and character. I highly recommend becoming the person that shows up the majority of the time.

Our neighbors recently invited us to their baby shower. We don't know them very well, even though we've lived on the same street for almost four years. In the last year, we have hung out a couple of times in an effort to build a relationship. The baby shower was 30 minutes away, and we could have easily declined. We didn't even think about not going.

I am so happy we went. We built trust, we got to meet new people, and, most importantly, it felt good to me. I think they were grateful and maybe a little surprised we went (I don't really know if that's true; I will ask!). Preston and I crave community. We have never had a solid group of friends that we hang out with, and some days it feels hard to create that. Why would I push away an opportunity to create connection when it's right in front of me?

Learning how to have difficult conversations is a frontier worth traversing. Successfully navigating them prevents us from getting stuck in our stories and opens us up to realities we only dream about. Realities where we can move forward, where we understand what's ours and what's someone else's, where we can let go of pleasing people, where we can express ourselves freely in a constructive way so we don't swallow anger and bitterness and resentment.

Let's imagine a hypothetical scenario. Three years ago, I had a weird conversation with a mum at my child's school—let's call her Mary. It feels tense between us. I decide that I don't like Mary, and I assume that Mary doesn't like me. I have no proof of how Mary feels. This is such an important example of the conclusions we jump to when we're not willing to lean in and look at our part.

Think about how often we play out scenarios like this because we don't have the skills to deal with our own discomfort and difficult conversations. It actually has nothing to do with Mary and everything to do with me. Sometimes, our instincts serve us well, and it's important to listen to them. And other times, we miss out on connection because of our own shortcomings.

At the end of the day, all we're doing here on earth is learning how to be in relationship with ourselves and one another. How we communicate through those difficult moments especially is a vital skill to being full of ourselves.

Perspective #1

Perspective is a word that means a lot to me. When we moved to Columbus, we bought a house in a popular neighborhood that is quirky, artsy, and charming. The house is 2,400 square feet, fully updated, and we paid $373,000 for it. At the time we purchased it, a gal I know said, "Oh, I know that area. What a great up-and-coming neighborhood." Her words baffled me. On what planet is ours an up-and-coming neighborhood? On what planet is $373,000 up-and-coming? We have nicely paved, tree-lined roads, lovely homes that are well-kept, low crime, and access to great amenities.

This gal lives in a ritzier neighborhood in Columbus, in a home valued at close to a million dollars. I appreciate that perspective is everything. From her life experience, I could see how our neighborhood could be described as up-and-coming, and yet her comment has stuck with me like glue. I checked my thinking. Was I offended by her comment? Did I feel like I was less than? A little. I also believe that her words are a great reminder of how important it is for me to stay in touch with reality.

When I first moved here, I loved America. The country where I could get anything and everything (except a good bra!). Today, I understand that we are not a country that admires peace and contentment, or one that recognizes that each person is inherently enough. The definition of "enough" is different for everyone, and yet this country tends to celebrate excess. A six- or seven-figure business is lauded as success—but what if someone is delighted with their five-figure business? What if someone adores their small house and isn't aiming to own a big one? Is that not success? Do we always have to want more?

I was watching *The Great British Bake Off* a couple of years ago, reminiscing about home while drooling over cakes and laughing over the antics of burnt sponges and failed designs. The talented bakers were competing for an engraved tray and an extended family picnic. That's it. And on one of the biggest television shows in the UK no less. Could you imagine telling potential contestants in America that they would be competing for a tray? It's unthinkable. The show would die before it even began. There would have to be a million-dollar prize, a book deal, their name in big lights, fireworks at the finale, and plenty of dramatic music. Forget good, old-fashioned camaraderie and a polite cheer.

America has little tolerance for small. Success is big and wild and the best. Americans proudly proclaim that their country is the world's biggest superpower. Heads up, we're not anymore. Americans proudly cheer on the "World Series." Fun fact, the only countries playing are America and Canada. American universities are revered like they are world-class institutions. That was certainly my experience at Texas A&M University. Guys, outside of the U.S., nobody has heard of Texas A&M University. In this regard, America can be terribly conceited, partly due to its size and lack of exposure to other cultures. As a European, America is incredibly insulated, largely because of its geography.

I want to remember what up-and-coming really means. Maybe I latched onto this gal's words too fiercely and she was using them more loosely. That could absolutely be true. Even if that's the case, I love the idea that I maintain a true perspective about my reality. Did you know that 60 percent of the world doesn't have a working toilet at home that properly manages human waste? Sixty percent! And in this country, a $373,000 home is "up-and-coming." What the fuck are we talking about? It's so easy for all of us, me included, to live in a suburban bubble and become oblivious to real problems.

I don't want to misunderstand what I have in a country where hitting a six-figure income is only the beginning of "making it." Believing that is not part of my value system. If you make six figures in a way that aligns with your values and creates meaning and purpose in your life, it's success every day of the week. It's bullshit if you think making six figures is what makes you successful, the very idea I have decided to unlearn.

It's also important for me to say that I love money. I think making lots of money is wonderful, and it has to be paired with something more meaningful to be truly gratifying. I'll prioritize successes every day that fulfill my requirement of being true to myself and remember that, in doing so, my success is as big as it gets.

Perspective #2

I've written a blog for a decade that has never had more than 275 subscribers. I have posted thoughtful content for 7+ years and have just broken the 1,000-follower mark. By every business coaching standard, I'm failing. And for so long, I believed that I was failing. Hence why I joined the mastermind. Hence why I felt like I wasn't good enough. What I wanted more than anything was to know myself well enough to find my definition of success and be comfortable with it.

I didn't know that serving a handful of clients was a success for me.

I didn't know that working 20 hours a week was what I really wanted.

I didn't know that making $14,000 in direct referrals in my first year of networking was a huge win.

I didn't know that making $1,000 in sales at my first speaking gig where I spoke for free was incredible.

I've spent 11 years as a coach grappling with and fighting for the perspective that my life is a roaring success. I now believe that to be true. Every single week, I touch approximately 135 people through my blog. About 56 percent read it, which is a kick-ass read rate. I learn from and grow with and pour into 7-10 clients every week in individual sessions. I provide a space where nine women get to explore confidence and success and their voice on their own terms in the Full of Herself Community. This reach is just the tip of the iceberg. That's 151 people every single week that are impacted by who I'm being—and I haven't mentioned my friends and family, strangers I meet, people who watch my Instagram reels, and on and on.

I am still learning how to grow my business (read: myself) to reach the clients I want to reach, and trust myself to be seen, to feel safe and worthy, and to serve well, all at the same time. Welcome to entrepreneurship. Some days, it feels like heaven. Other days, it feels like a cluster. I don't think that will ever change. I don't think it's supposed to. What is changing is the nurturing relationship I have with myself to meet life's challenges with grace. Age is a glorious companion in that sense.

The healing never stops. This work of understanding how to be in a relationship with oneself and others never stops. We have dark spots, we have conversations unfinished, we have sorrowful memories. Our job is to clean up our mess. If there is a moment in your life that you ruminate on, I would suggest that you look at it more closely.

What do you need to work through—say, let go of—with a coach, counselor, mentor, or therapist so that your energy can be put to better use? It's not kind to yourself to waste your energy ruminating. It gets in the way of your light shining even more brightly.

How Often Do You Say No?

Reposted from mooresoulsessions.com/blog
How Often Do You Say No? May 26, 2022

Is there a dream you have for your life? An idea that's been sitting with you for weeks, years, or decades?

Something you envisage creating, somewhere you want to live, a skill you want to acquire?

Among many dreams, one that's prominent for me right now is writing a book.

I have started writing her, I am finding my way with her—or maybe she's finding her way with me—and I am committed to finishing her.

Please email me and cheer me on.

I have started saying no to most things that don't support this effort.

In particular, I said no to a panel that I was asked to speak on. While it would support my other goal of growing the community, I had to admit that I am spreading myself too thin.

Until now, I've tended to say yes to most everything, with some discernment, because the entrepreneurial journey has required that of me in a lot of ways.

I'm seeing clearly that I can't focus on growing the community and writing my book, *at the same time.* I will run myself ragged in the process.

That said, it's always both. I will never stop growing the community because it means so much to me, and I know it's a powerful place for women to experience the change they desire. If it's in the natural course of a moment to invite someone to the community, I want to do so.

Sure, the panel is one hour of my time. I could have said yes, and doing so would not have been a bad decision.

What's more true for me is that I have a finite amount of creativity and energy, and I want to spend it where it counts the most right now: on my book.

So, *Full of Herself* (that's her name), it's you and me, baby. [Insert coy giggle.]

I think "no" is a valuable tool in your arsenal. Use it with discernment, and you'll start to enjoy saying it because it could provide tangible evidence that you're on your way to your dreams becoming a reality.

With love,

Sarah
x

Favorite Coaching Questions/Statements

These are my favorites because they are both introspective and action-oriented in nature. Some of them help to determine and clarify the gap being addressed in coaching rather than rushing in to "fix" the problem which is a mistake many coaches make.

These questions have the power to stop my clients in their tracks and make them think. We take for granted that we know how to define simple concepts. For example, we think we know what success means or what confidence means, and yet defining them requires some thought. That intentional thought helps shape the decisions we make, and, as a result, we can then start to become more conscious creators of our lives.

If more people asked thoughtful questions like these, our connections would be deeper and our judgments lessened.

- There are 7.7 billion people on this planet. On a scale of 1 - 7.7 billion, where would you rank your overall happiness and success? (Thanks to Gary Vaynerchuck for this question.)[17]

- What would you like to have happen? (Thanks to Fred Kofman for this question, which he stated during a program I attended. Most coaches hear a client's issue and then dive right into working through it. Fred taught me that it's important to ask

---

[17] Gary Vaynerchuck, *Twelve and a Half: Leveraging the Emotional Ingredients Necessary for Business Success*, 1st ed. (New York: Harper Business, 2021), 3.

this question first to see where the client wants to go. It's a great question for any conversation.)

- How does that make you feel?

- What he/she thinks of you is none of your business.

- What do you think?

- Why haven't you created the future you want already?

- Are you in agreement with that feedback/idea/train of thought? (Especially important when the other person is an authority figure, like a boss, because we tend to give them too much power. A boss is a fallible human, too.)

- What's your definition of success?

- What is the situation here to teach you about yourself?

- What are your core values?

- Give me an example of how you lived into your value/your definition of success this week.

- Talk to me about your reflection time this week.

- There's nothing to figure out.

- How can you engage your body in the healing process?

- What was most valuable about this session?

- What commitment would you like to make to yourself this week?

- What's your story of why _____ isn't happening?

- What can you learn for next time?

- What could you have done differently?

- Your thoughts aren't wrong. They are incomplete.

- Thank you.

- I believe you.

Quick Guide to Words

Words impact our behaviors and our outcomes. There are some common words we use unconsciously that do not serve us. In the spirit of adoring words, I'd like to share some substitutions for your consideration. When we take the time to think about the reality we're creating with our words and make some tweaks, we can raise our consciousness and sense of agency. I recommend striving to use these suggestions at least 30 percent more often.

I should → I could, I want to, I don't want to, I choose to, I get to.

"Should" implies burden and a lack of agency. When you drop "should," your language becomes less negative and more neutral. The truth is, if you're not living your life as a victim you get to choose and own that decision. Take charge of your choices.

> I should work out. → I get to work out. I could work out.

> I should go to bed earlier. → I don't want to go to bed earlier.

"Could," "want to," "choose to," and "get to" indicate that you are actively creating *your* life.

I need to → I could, I want to, I don't want to, I choose to, I get to.

You don't need to do anything. Even paying taxes. You choose to pay taxes because it's the lawful thing to do and part of being a responsible citizen. If you don't choose to do something, you are communicating that you are comfortable with the outcome of not doing said thing. So, it's still a choice. Choose agency.

But → And.

As you may have already noticed, I have made a number of choices throughout this book to use "and" instead of "but." It's intentional. Try it out, and see how your perspective shifts.

I don't have time → I don't want to, It's not a priority.

"I don't have time" is an easy lie. Once again, it allows us to be passive, to blame rather than speak in a way that puts us at the center of our decision-making.

Not having time to work out isn't the same as not making time for it. *I know it's important, and I'm not making it a priority* is a far more energizing statement than, *I don't have time.* Don't be scared of your truth. If you want to be magnetic, start talking in a way most people don't. Most people talk as if things are happening to them.

The greater truth is that things are happening—period. In order to make sense of the world, we then get to decide, is it happening *to* me or *for* me? We make it about us because that's how we relate to the world around us. News flash: most things don't happen to us unless we let them.

Can't → Can

In terms of neutral thinking, "I can't" would be an example of negativity. Nobody wants to hear a can't-baby. Jeez, my six-year-old says it enough. Maybe he says it because I say it more than I think I do.

What *can* you do?

You can say sorry to your spouse for micro-managing their mornings with the kids.

You can speak up to senior leadership about the lack of a plan during a massive organizational change.

You can start bragging with your kids.

You can tell your colleagues that you need to hop off this meeting, even though it's going over, to be on time for your next meeting.

While there are things you will never be able to do, focus on what you can, that which is within your control.

Avoid Right/Wrong and Best/Worst

I think we're too quick to judge what is right and wrong. Do right and wrong exist if what's right to me is wrong to you? Is this the right decision or the best I have *right now*? Right/wrong and best/worst put too much pressure on ourselves. Clients will often ask me, "Did I do the right thing?" or, "Do you think I handled it wrong?" I often say, "I don't know. What do you think?," and then I remind them that right and wrong are made-up constructs. Intention is everything.

As someone recovering from self-judgment, these questions are more helpful for me:

Was what I said/did in alignment for me?

Do I feel at peace?

Is there anything more I can say or do?

What did I learn?

Knowing that my best is different every day, did I do my best in that moment?

By the way, I don't subscribe to the moniker, "Be better than you were yesterday." What horseshit. This implies that growth is linear, which it's not. My best tomorrow might be worse than my best today because of a million circumstances—and it's still good enough.

No and Yes

You are entitled to say no. No can be a full sentence. It *is* a full sentence. Although I'm a fan of "No, thank you," you don't have to explain yourself to anyone ever. It might be polite to do so and create connection in the relationship. I'm all for that. Just know that, despite every urge in your body and mind to explain yourself, an explanation is optional.

Please start saying no.

If you feel overloaded, you can say no to taking on anything else.

If you don't want to organize the group, you can say, "No, thank you."

If you sent the emails on behalf of everyone last year and don't want to do it again this year, even though people will assume you will, you can say, "No thanks."

If you don't want to cook for the third night in a row, you can say, "Nope, not tonight people."

In fact, I'd go a step further and say it's your responsibility to say no. Otherwise, everyone suffers, and you suffer the most. We're talking about self-awareness and boundaries. That's why doing *your work* is so important. If you don't sit down and take the time to reflect on why you're banging around the kitchen or resenting your partner, you don't get any closer to knowing that "no" could be an option. Instead, you stay in people-pleasing mode, which looks glitzy from the outside and is soul-sucking on the inside.

We all love to love people who help people. Most of the time, in my experience, the help isn't altruistic. It's code for, "I haven't done my work." The following thoughts may arise:

I'm too afraid to look inside myself so I'll keep helping you, and then I'll secretly become resentful of you for not helping me in return. Or, I generally feel unloved and unseen. I'll keep a lid on that because I get love and attention from helping so it's better to keep suffering to feel a boost of self-esteem from how people view me. Meanwhile, I don't know how the hell to help myself and my life's a mess.

Learn to help yourself. Stop and assess what your needs are, and then practice communicating them. Those are two separate skills.

Most of the confusion and frustration that we experience isn't about the no itself. It's about the fact that we don't know what our boundaries are and how to clearly communicate them. Instead, we over-promise, procrastinate, say nothing, waffle, blame, hide, yell, become distant, eat too much, point the finger, distract ourselves—anything to avoid being with and telling the truth.

Don't let that be you.

Run your thinking and your needs past your coach, sponsor, mentor, or therapist to make sure you're not tricking yourself (we're very good at that). When you're clear, share what you need and keep it simple.

All of this can apply to saying "yes" as well. Perhaps you don't know how to accept help. Perhaps you like to get things done on your own because you think you do them best. Perhaps you were taught not to rely on anyone else. Boundaries are still at play here. You don't know how to loosen up and let people in yet. Whatever the reason, "Yes, please" can be a full sentence, too.

Would you like my help? Yes, please.

Can I help you? Yes, that would be great.

What can I bring tonight? Sodas and napkins would be great (a form of yes).

We all love to be helpful, so when you say "yes," you give someone else the gift of being able to contribute. You also create intimacy.

Sometimes all you need to say is "no, thank you," and "yes, please" to feel at peace. Peace is your birthright, and what God wants for you. Peace is who you were born to be.

As I've shared, I really do believe that words matter. While these language tweaks may seem minor, they add up to big results over time. They build a picture of a person who calls their shots, who actively engages in their life, and who creates room for duality.

Doing the Hardest Thing First

I once heard someone say that procrastination occurs in the absence of a dream.

Procrastination and not feeling productive are struggles I hear women talk about relatively often. We have so many competing demands—careers, parenting, taking care of our homes, taking care of ourselves—that can leave us feeling paralyzed, burned out, and unsure of who to be and what to do next.

Here's my antidote to procrastination and lack of productivity. I'm very clear that one dream I yearn to fulfill daily is to feel proud of myself. What helps me feel proud is doing the hardest thing first. I find that I tend to procrastinate less when I take this approach because I get to experience myself as capable so early on in my day. When I feel capable, I feel proud and my possibilities open up even more.

Let's define a hard thing. For me, a hard thing might be something I'm scared of, like picking up the phone to say I'm sorry because I was unkind. Perhaps it's a task that will take the longest, like filling out a detailed speaker application. Perhaps I don't know how to do it, so it feels daunting, like gathering my tax information. Perhaps it's easy and I don't want to do it, like vacuuming. I don't judge the reason that it feels like the hardest task. I accept how I feel about it, and if it's very important to me and not a distraction from the real work at hand, I get to work.

I've gotten good at doing whatever is hard, even if I'm not very good at the task itself. Doing the hardest thing first is a strategy for raising my self-esteem because I am able to look at myself in a mirror and see a woman who reflects back strength. A woman who does hard things day in, day out.

Horse Bully

My beloved pony Raffles and I were a dynamic duo for years. When we first got him, my legs came midway down his belly. As the years went on, I grew into him, literally, and we grew into each other, figuratively. He was an older boy and, together, we went charging around the countryside. My job was to hang on, maintain just enough control, and point him in the right direction. Raffles' job was to jump and run free.

After Raffles died, if I wanted to keep riding, which I couldn't have imagined not doing, my only option was our other horse, Barney. Barney was a totally different kettle of fish. He was a lot younger and needed a lot of training. Mum had bought Barney for both of us, but I never anticipated being the one to train him. I thought Raffles and I would have many great years together. I didn't want to train a new horse. I didn't feel entirely comfortable with Barney's size. If you know anything about horses, Raffles' and Barney's heights were 13.2 and 16.2, respectively. Put it this way: Raffles was an average-sized pony, and Barney was a big horse.

Where Raffles was solid and reliable, Barney was more temperamental. He was very sweet and I loved him, and he had some quirks. He had more of a nervous disposition and would sometimes buck me off even going into a simple canter. We couldn't figure out what was causing him to buck, and naturally, I started to feel nervous when I rode him. Horses, like most animals, are very sensitive to energy. I wonder if Barney's bucking was a response to my own emotional baggage.

Since he was so big, I often had trouble putting on his bridle—although his size wasn't the only factor. We would wrestle and tug back and forth with me standing on my tiptoes on an overturned feed bucket trying to reach up over his ears. He would fling his head back and forth. It was an exhausting debacle. I would spend over an hour trying to get the bridle on with no luck.

I became so enraged that my time was being wasted over such a small task. I would yell and scream, hoping nobody heard me, which, for the most part, they didn't because we lived in the country. We did live right next to a church, and I'm sure one or two churchgoers heard my antics, which immediately made me feel ashamed, and I zipped it.

There were several times when I hit Barney's neck with my fists in total desperation. Not super hard, but certainly enough to make an impact. *All I want to do is go out on a ride. Why aren't you cooperating? Why are we wasting time on this stupid bridle? We could have been back by now, and instead, we're still standing here. Why are you doing this to me?*

I felt helpless. Helplessness is the root of depression. I shared with you earlier that when I was diagnosed with depression, I felt fairly certain that I had struggled with it on and off my whole life and didn't know. I believe some depression was at play during my teenage years. There were certainly tumultuous times due to my dad's drinking, the constant yo-yo-ing of friends in and out of my life, and our overall family dynamic with half-siblings who all had stories and trauma of their own.

The irony is that I was bullied, and I went on to bully my horse. My childhood bullies incorrectly and prematurely accused me of abusing my horse at age 11. Yet by the time I was 15, Barney became a target of my frustrations. I'm sorry, Barney. You deserved better. Despite my shortcomings, I also think I loved you well. It can be both.

Lake House

Finding our lake house was a gift from God. We bought a house in a town that I hadn't even spent 24 hours in when I found it.

2022 was Austin's first real summer holiday, having just finished kindergarten. In an effort to keep him busy, I booked a week away for the two of us to Lake Erie. I didn't think Lake Erie was particularly nice, having visited it a couple of different times. I thought it was brown and overrated. Nevertheless, because it was close and I wanted to get to know our state of Ohio better, I booked a week at an inexpensive Airbnb in a town called Fairport Harbor. I had never heard of Fairport Harbor. I chose it because it's by the lake, has a beach and a lighthouse, and seemed cute enough. I didn't have any expectations for the trip except that I knew we could make our own fun.

As soon as I drove into town, I was taken by its charm. It was quiet and had a cute little downtown. The beach was lovely with lots of amenities, and I was delighted that the water wasn't brown but actually quite clear. On our first morning, I rented a golf cart. Austin and I went cruising around town and low-and-behold, I saw a house for sale.

As I was driving past the house, I realized it had a view of the lake. I stopped. With my curiosity piqued, I called the realtor and asked about the price. It was in our budget. I couldn't believe it. A house with a view of the lake within our budget? Thirty minutes later, after returning the golf cart, Austin and I were taking a tour of the inside. I loved it. After over three weeks of negotiations, we landed on a number, and the house is now ours.

What I love most about this story is that I was willing to take action when the opportunity presented itself. This story feels very similar to our moving-to-Columbus story. From these two experiences, I learned that checking things off my bucket list is fairly easy and doable when I put my mind and energy into it.

This doesn't mean I start forcing solutions. There have certainly been many times that I've wrestled, micromanaged, and forced something to fruition that wasn't in alignment. Those experiences were painful. Even in the moments where I did succeed in making them happen, they never satiated the hole inside of me. If anything, those holes got bigger. I was disillusioned because the thing I thought I wanted and needed actually made me feel worse.

Instead, I do my best to get clear about what I want, I consistently orient myself toward it, and I let it find me. In other words, when I allow God to work with my desires, things happen easily, and I am able to delight in their timing. I had no idea these opportunities would await me. Because I had been doing *my work* (it always comes back to self-awareness), I could trust myself to see them and seize them.

Life is a heck of an adventure, and it's amazing what comes my way when I'm busy living.

Whispers

I'm brilliant at following my curiosity. That year I stepped away from coaching, explored doing a Ph.D., took an insurance job, and worked in real estate? When I was finishing my master's degree hoping to become a travel writer, and I decided to work in lingerie? When I said, let's put an offer on a lake house in a town that I had spent one day in? When I got the invitation to fly to America on a whim after finishing university in the UK?

Every single one of those moments was an intentional decision to scratch an itch. What I would call a whisper. An idea came to me, my curiosity was piqued, and I wanted to see where the road could lead me. I have become an expert in exploring these whispers. I feel strongly that I owe it to myself to listen closely to them and take action, if any is necessary. When I do, I don't have to look back and think, *What if?*

I have honed this skill of listening to whispers over time. Now, after years of trial and error, I'm clear that when I get an idea, I need to give myself the space to hear it and digest it, and then ask myself if there's a next step.

Let's say I have the whisper that I'd like to work for an organization, and I decide I'm going to reach out to have a conversation. I try not to start by talking to myself or others about how great this partnership could be, the money that could be involved, how great it could look on my resumé, how it's a natural next step based on what I've done to date, etc. It's very easy for me to get ahead of myself and assign too much meaning to a simple email or phone call.

My commitment to myself, in this instance, is to stay in the outreach effort and see what happens next. If I get a response, awesome. If I still feel energized and would like to set a meeting, I ask for one. If it starts to feel hard to coordinate our schedules, I might reevaluate and say this isn't worth it. I might also be tenacious and keep pushing forward. It all depends on my energy. If I'm excited then I'm unlikely to become drained. If I'm frustrated, then the situation is taking a toll on me, and I may need to adjust my expectations, or I may need to recognize that I'm pushing too much.

When I say energy, I am not talking about whether I feel like doing something. I'm talking about my level of enthusiasm and positive expectation. I keep going in this fashion, step by step, moment by moment, until I run out of next steps. I have a penchant for making a situation bigger than it is because I want to feel bigger than I am. Focusing on my energy helps me to go with the flow and keeps me humble, or as we say in the program, "right-sized."

Sometimes an idea comes to me, and I don't know what the next step is. Often this feels like a relief because it's one less thing I have to think about. I can let it sit and marinate. I have learned that just because an idea comes to me doesn't mean now is the time to take action. Thank you to my friend and talented coach, Cara Viana, for teaching me this valuable lesson.

I no longer have to waste my time pushing boulders uphill, struggling, sweating, breathing like I'm about to die, and hating every minute of it. I can let time and energy work in my favor. I can let the whisper come to me. When energy and inspiration strike, I can take action. Action doesn't have to be linear. I can take one step immediately because it seems like the next right thing to do and then wait for six months until it's clear what's next.

A whisper can sit with us for years, decades even, and sometimes it can be achieved in a matter of minutes when we understand the energetic interplay at hand. Sometimes a whisper folds. It's a nonstarter or, more painfully, it almost launches and then comes to a crash. I am very clear that every experience is valuable because I explored it and learned more about myself and the world in the process. In that sense, listening to a whisper is never a waste of time, and it keeps me from feeling regret.

Logically, I would never dream of beating myself up because something didn't work out. I do, however, beat myself up because I'm disappointed. I'm learning slowly how to reach for a better thought than, *What did I do wrong?* In those moments, I feel all the appropriate feelings of rage and grief and bewilderment and fear over the loss of what could have been. What's most true is that I'm fixated on what I think the outcome should be, and I'm unwilling to be flexible. In those moments of desperation, the whisper whispers that I must trust the process.

There could be a million reasons that something doesn't work out. Take, for example, a job that I want and don't get. On the surface I am disappointed, and then when I think about it, maybe I have dodged a bullet. Perhaps one person would have been difficult to work with, negatively impacting my energy and therefore many areas of my life. Maybe my sleep would have suffered because the work was more complex than I realized. Maybe somebody else needed to shine in this role much more than me. Perhaps they wouldn't pay me on time (I've had this experience). Perhaps I wouldn't have been very good at the work, and I would have been forcing myself, a round peg, into a square hole. Instead of focusing on what should have been mine, I find it helpful to remember that if I didn't get it, it wasn't mine to get in the first place.

I don't want to sugarcoat the many reasons that life takes unexpected turns. Instead, I am applying a meaning that helps me, that works in my favor so I can keep moving forward rather than getting stuck. I know that things tend to work out in my favor when I trust the way my life unfolds.

Generally speaking, because I am so driven by thinking big, I feel an immense amount of pride when I give myself permission to listen to the whisper in the first place.

Sometimes the whisper becomes exactly what I thought it would be, and I say, "Hallelujah! Thank you, Jesus." Although, in these instances, what I learn about myself is seldom what I thought it would be. When I signed up to study to be a life coach, I thought I would walk away with tools and techniques to coach other people. Never did I expect I would first have to test them out on myself. As a result, I grew immensely over the course of that year of studying. It's fun to listen to a whisper and see who I become through my willingness to take action.

I love the word whisper because, for me, it implies that it's coming from somewhere else, someone else. Something greater than me whispers in my soul. For me, that's God. This brings me great comfort because trying to run the show alone is boring, lonely, and way too hard.

Depression Day In, Day Out

Reposted from mooresoulsessions.com/blog
What a Saturday That Was (original title), August 25, 2022

On Saturday, I felt so depressed. It came seemingly out of nowhere. I woke up feeling good, had taken Austin to open his own bank account, and once we got home, I felt sad and low.

One of my mentors reminded me that it's important to parent myself, to not let myself descend into helplessness.

I didn't want to have to do more things to help myself. *Are you kidding me? Don't I do enough already? Why can't I just wake up and feel normal?*

And because I've been here 100 times before, my body remembered that the pain of not helping myself is far worse than the pain of being responsible.

I tidied my room. I cried on Preston's shoulder and got honest about what I was feeling. I journaled. I called my Al-Anon sponsor. I read my daily readings. I stretched and did foam-rolling exercises. I left a message for a friend in response to something hard she was going through. And I started some forgiveness work around the lie I believe about myself, "There is something wrong with me."

Maybe it was the realization of that lie that made me feel topsy-turvy. My body knew it could no longer hide that truth and needed to recalibrate. I'm not sure, and it makes sense.

I'm proud that I parented myself well and recognized where my behavior was unmanageable.

I want to remember to parent myself well and know that there is power in my powerlessness.

With love,

Sarah x

Not So Different

A close friend once told me, "Sarah, maybe you're not that unique." I told her that "I am unique" and "like to do things differently," and she shrugged. I felt put out by her lack of a response, and it has stuck with me for years.

Of course, I'm unique. I moved to the U.S. with $100 in my pocket and little to no plan. I bought my first house as a foreclosure because I'm real estate savvy. I spent my childhood traveling the world. Don't you know I have thousands of coaching hours under my belt? Listen to my accent. Of course, I'm different.

What I didn't know is that I was actually saying, *If I'm not unique, who am I?*

When we want to believe something, or better yet refute it, we can find all the data we need to back up our truth.

Today, I think my friend is right. While I do believe my life experiences are unique, I'm clear that I'm not unique. I'm a human with emotions and struggles, just like you. I'm doing my best to be a version of myself that's in alignment with my gifts and ideas. I'm trying to live a meaningful life, be in good relationships with the people that matter to me, say sorry when I mess up, and contribute to my community—all universal desires.

What excites me as I write this is that I no longer want to be unique. What I want most is to be at peace. I am special, *and* I'm not unique. I believe that to be true now. It can be both.

The Work Is Not Done

When you possess a growth mindset, you're actively seeking out opportunities for learning and expansion. A growth mindset is your best friend. A fixed mindset is dangerous.

I was in a fixed mindset when I was experiencing depression and suicidal thinking. I couldn't see other solutions. I felt trapped. Evidence of a fixed mindset comes in the form of finite statements about yourself that imply you have your life or some situation figured out. Let me share some examples.

"I used to be so selfish. I'm not anymore." *Until you have a child who doesn't want to share, and it triggers old feelings.*

"I finally figured out my control issues." *Well, why does Gina bother you so much? Is it because she's controlling?*

"There's no point in moving companies. I'd never get the job anyway." *Until you become burned out and resentful at your current company and need to take a leave of absence to feel somewhat human again.*

What's more true than the "I have it all figured out" sentiment is, "I have figured *something* out." You've had a breakthrough. That's reason to be proud. That's growth. And, you have not arrived.

I'm sharing this reminder because my clients who are newer to coaching don't yet understand the nuanced experience of having a growth mindset. We are setting ourselves up for disappointment when we think we have entirely overcome something. We end up feeling surprised and shocked when the same problem raises its head two weeks later or two decades later. We find ourselves saying, "I thought I dealt with this," unknowingly shaming ourselves for the continued struggle.

We like to think we've dealt with something because we put forth some effort at the time and got some resolution. Our meaning-making brains love a neat and tidy explanation. That's where I come in. As your coach, I remind you that being messy is part of the process and that this is a step, not the whole staircase. I find comfort in my own words because I want to hear them too.

Growth is about context. When I feel depressed, is it helpful or hurtful to me to question why I'm struggling when I thought I put depression to bed years ago? It's hurtful because it keeps me stuck in a fixed mindset. With a growth mindset, I might ask myself, *What's been happening in the last couple of weeks that could have contributed to this feeling today?* We are never the same at any given moment because life, like us, is always changing.

For example, I might feel safe eating the way I do and feel like I've got a handle on it, finally. Then I go on holiday, and I'm resentful because I want to eat like everybody else. This happens because I decide to believe the fantasy that other people can eat whatever they like and feel great when the truth is I have no idea how they feel. *If they can do it, so can I,* I think. So I dive right in. A few days later, feeling like crap, I say to myself, *Again, really?* Or, maybe I'm relaxed in my career and, at home, I'm a drill sergeant. We can figure something out in one area and be surprised or even in denial that it pops up in another.

I think it's more helpful to think about life—even lessons learned that seem like I have it all figured out when I don't—as landing points. Each time something new comes up or I'm triggered by something, it's an opportunity to learn. With a growth mindset, I'm rooted in the belief that my work is never done. I can be delighted that I figured something out in the past knowing that growth and experience will support me for the next round of learning. This approach is a more honest representation of the cyclical nature of life and growth.

You Never Know

I've always been attracted to power. Part of that is because I feel powerless, and not in the best sense of the word. For example, I hear the word lawyer, and I immediately think, *Oooh, fancy.* You might respond that way to a founder or a nurse, someone who wears a Rolex, or your neighbor who is building a new in-ground swimming pool.

In part, my response puts that lawyer on a pedestal and is rooted in my struggle to feel equal to others. I have often in my life felt either above or below people. That belief, even when it arises, hangs around for a lot less time these days, which is a marker of great growth for me. When I have a thought that is hurtful to me, I'm far less concerned about having had the thought and much more interested in how long it hangs around and its subsequent impact. If the impact is negligible, I keep it moving. In that respect, the thought itself doesn't define me.

Last week, Preston was telling me that a lawyer he met was experiencing paranoia and was drinking and drugging heavily. His family was moving out of their family home. In that moment—and I have these moments over and over again—I was surprised to hear about his mental health struggles because I associate his fancy job title with somehow being "superior."

Yet again, I was reminded that I never know what's going on in anyone's life. I don't need to feel small, even a smidge, because of the story I've made up about who they are. Everyone struggles. I know this intellectually, and I do not know it in my bones, yet, because I keep feeling surprised and delighted when I hear such stories. I long for the day when I hear a story like this one and immediately think something like, "How hard." Right now, it takes me a few seconds or minutes to get there. I'm proud that I get there.

Then, the little cogs in my brain start to make sense of it all with thoughts like these: *I can rest a little easier. Sarah, you never know. Stop judging your insides with someone else's outsides. Yeah, he can struggle, too. Hmm, that's surprising. Oh, that's right, there's nothing to chase. I'm successful, too. Shit, I'm doing better than he is, even though I thought he was doing better than me. Sarah, you never know.*

Did you notice how my better-than thinking crept into the process of understanding and healing when I said, "I'm doing better than he is …"? It's not ideal, and I'm ok with it. My body is still trying to digest the idea that I'm equal to everyone.

Brand New Day

A brilliant friend of mine once told me that she lives her life creating brand new days. She doesn't want a repeat of yesterday, a half-assed version of Tuesday two weeks ago, or Christmas to be like it was 10 years ago. What happened yesterday has nothing to do with today. She wants today to be a brand new day. She shared with me that her second husband died many years ago and today, when people ask her about her relationship status, she says she is single. My mind was blown. I thought, *You don't say you're a widow. Wow. How novel.*

She told me that, at first, during the most acute period of her grief, she described herself as a widow until she realized that her motive for doing so was manipulative. She enjoyed the sympathy and pity and extra attention that came her way. Until she didn't. She decided to make a change in her language. To this day she tells people that she is single and says that most people assume she is divorced. It's interesting what we assume.

For her, this way of answering is an example of how she is creating a brand new day. She loves her husband and the memories of their life. It's not that it's too painful to mention his name, it's that the word widow keeps her rooted in the past and doesn't serve the blank slate of today and all of its possibilities. Today cannot be a brand new day if we intentionally put the past in it.

The word widow, to me, feels so different from the word single. Widow feels like a heavier word; sad, mourning, off limits. Single feels freer, more optimistic, ready for something.

The decision to say single is a paradigm shift for me. I thought widow meant honoring the memory of her husband. It's also the truth. Aren't we supposed to speak the truth? I'm pretty sure I would have chosen the word widow. *Yes, I might be technically single but really I'm a widow.* I realize using the word widow can be an example of playing the victim. Victimhood is so enticing. Stories like this one pop up regularly in my life, showing me how much I love to be a victim. I then choose to bask in the opportunity to shift my victimhood one tiny moment at a time.

As I was listening to her story, I also thought about the degree to which I do not live in today. When Preston and I first met, I asked him how he would rate me on a scale of 1-10. His answer was seven. I don't know where I rate myself on the scale, and we can all agree that this is a misguided answer to the woman you love. No question about that. That said, I don't remember any context, and I don't like my question. It's a question rooted in insecurity that feels like a set-up.

As my friend was sharing her story with me, I thought about the absurdity of how I had been feeling resentful about Preston rating me as a seven. Preston said this approximately 16 years ago. *Sixteen years* for God's sake. I can be fully present one moment, and then play tug-of-war with a scenario from two decades ago like it's nothing. Today, I have a keen awareness of which thoughts serve me and which don't, and I can see and accept my humanity in both. I'm trying out the approach of a *brand new day*, and all the serenity it has to offer me.

Faith

During COVID, I started going to church for the first time in my life. I love the look on Christians' faces when they hear I didn't grow up in the church. It's similar to how I feel when someone I'm talking to reveals that they haven't left the country they were born in. While I wasn't seeking out a church per se, I was seeking out more spirituality and more of a relationship with God.

At the first service I attended, I broke down crying when the band began to play. I didn't know how much my soul craved connection and belonging in a big room with others until that moment. I found myself saying, *I can't believe I go to church.* Am I one of *those* people? Those Christians I judged? I love aging because I get to become someone I judged.

Someone at church once asked me, "How do you define faith?" My immediate answer was, "As an adventure." I feel so lucky that I wasn't raised in the church, that I don't have years of hurt to deconstruct. I'm coming in with this relatively clean slate, barring my own judgments, and getting to explore what faith means for me. I don't identify as a Christian. I am not a follower of Jesus, and I don't read the Bible or attend Bible study.

I kept saying things like, "I'm new to this," and, "I don't know much about God and Christianity," and, "I don't know what I'm talking about." In some instances that is very true. In others, I caught myself and thought, *Hey, Sarah, you know a lot more than you're allowing space for. Your relationship with God is very familiar.* With that realization, I smiled and was able to stop apologizing for what I don't know (putting my fixed mindset in the past), and open up to that which I'm curious about (embracing a growth mindset).

I do believe that if your pastor, your church, or your family tells you that a certain way is the right way, then the whole point of faith has been missed. To be dictated to is not a recipe for feeling full of yourself, for exploration, for joy, for meaning, for change. I think that if you have doubts, you're doing it right. It's through your doubts and questions that your faith expands.

When you believe without questioning, I'd propose that you aren't a believer at all. You've simply arrived at a point where you think that you've engineered uncertainty out of your life—nothing could misdefine faith more than that. That shit will reemerge somewhere, and it will stink to high heaven. Humans live cyclically, such as with the seasons. If there is no room to evolve, whether spiritually, financially, or in any area of our lives, I'm not interested. What is faith if it's not uncertainty, the very breath that brings adventure to life?

Recently, while working my Al-Anon program with my sponsor, I defined faith in this way: Faith means not being able to see or understand how something will work out and proceeding with the peace that it will. Faith also means being surprised and delighted by how things might turn out. A bit like, "Ooooh, what does God have in store for me with this?"

As I become more spiritual, I understand how central faith is to my life. If I am not taking care of my spiritual condition and accepting uncertainty, nothing else thrives. Not my health, relationships, body, work, creativity, finances, or ability to have fun. Nothing.

In that sense, I seem to be talking more about spirituality and faith with my clients than ever before. I emphasize so deeply to them that they aren't engaging with their spirit and faith if they're not taking time to reflect on intimate thoughtful questions, such as: who they are, what they're thinking and feeling, what's working and what isn't, what needs their attention and what has too much, what they fear and desire, and what they need to let go of. All of these questions develop the spirit that is you. The way we develop faith in ourselves is through the faith to let go. We feel safe enough to let go when we believe that something greater than ourselves is at play.

Imagine reviewing your life holistically using the Full of Herself Wheel. While spirituality is one of many elements on the wheel, I believe it's best placed at the center of mine. Spirituality is the support beam upon which every other area of my life rests. Think about what is at the center of yours, and if it is serving you.

I no longer attend church as I believe our values are misaligned, and I'm very grateful for the experience. I love my ever-evolving adventure with faith because with it I seem to reach for ease more than I reach for figuring it out.

Amen.

Why I Love Being Married to an Addict[18]

Addicts are self-centered to the core. They're "driven by one hundred forms of fear"[19]—it says so in the Big Book of Alcoholics Anonymous. At the same time, they are often incredibly charismatic, fun, and gregarious.

My addict, Preston, fits this description perfectly.

When I met my husband 17 years ago, I was 22 years old.

I didn't know a thing about addiction.

And yet, during a two-hour car ride where he was held captive, I determinedly proclaimed that he was crazy and wrong for thinking he could possibly be one of "those people."

"Why do you insist on degrading yourself by calling yourself an addict?" I asked. "You've been clean for five years. Why do you still think you're an addict?"

His response?

"I don't have a problem calling myself that. You do."

---

[18] Sarah T. Moore, "Why I Love Being Married to an Addict," Medium, Recovery International, April 21, 2020, https://medium.com/recovery-international/why-i-love-being-married-to-an-alcoholic-e296250da60e.

[19] *Alcoholics Anonymous Big Book*, 4th ed. (New York: Alcoholics Anonymous World Services, 2002), 62.

I was infuriated and disappointed in him.

If only he could see I was right.

I continued to berate him, genuinely believing he would see the light. In my mind, alcoholics were waste-of-space, couldn't-get-it-together, had-themselves-to-blame drunks who drank out of brown paper bags.

What I know today is something quite different.

I have learned that addiction is absolutely not a choice. It is a disease, like cancer or diabetes. You may find yourself rejecting that idea immediately. There is no rejecting it. It's a fact as outlined by the American Medical Association in 1956. Addicts are not hopeless idiots who have no willpower and should make better choices. Let me repeat. This has nothing to do with willpower. Addicts are men and women like you and me who are suffering from a disease that is chronic, incurable, and fatal.

The disease of addiction is a progressive disease, which means it only gets worse over time and people who are active in their addiction are at risk of dying prematurely. The hope is to become aware of it, live with it, and manage it through a 12-step program like Alcoholics Anonymous (AA) or Narcotics Anonymous (NA). Once an addict is in recovery, they still consider themselves an addict. No one becomes fully "recovered." They are forever, with God's grace, "recovering."

One of the most intriguing facts about the disease of addiction is that it's one of the few diseases that make you believe there's nothing wrong with you, as if you don't have a disease at all. When you have cancer, there's no debating it. When you have heart disease, you accept that you have heart disease. Yet, so often with addiction and mental illness, people believe they don't have the illness. That's why this disease is described as cunning and baffling. Addicts need our compassion and the necessary services to recover.

I wish to be a part of a society where addiction is supported, not scorned, and where we talk about it openly.

The first time I went to one of Preston's 12-step meetings, in a small Texas town, all my assumptions were confirmed. I had come face-to-face with the underlings of society. About 80 percent of the men and women at this meeting were getting papers signed. When I found out these papers were for their parole officers and halfway houses, I felt scared and utterly curious.

I'd never met anyone who had been arrested, let alone gone to jail.

My thoughts turned to this new man I was falling in love with.

How could I be attracted to someone who felt so at home here?

I was scared of what I didn't know.

Have you ever heard that when you point your finger at someone, you have three fingers pointing back at yourself? "Let me change him so I can feel better" is not a 12-step principle.

As I learned more about addiction, I learned that I had been sur-rounded by the disease my whole life. This came as a complete surprise because what I knew was normal. If people didn't drink and party, I thought they were losers and weird. Conversely, I didn't know the emotional pain and suffering I was feeling as a 22-year-old was a direct result of the alcoholism in my family.

What do I mean by emotional pain and suffering? I didn't feel quite right in myself. I didn't have the long-lasting friendships that I desper-ately wanted. I would argue with Preston for what seemed like an eter-nity. Just as arguments were finishing, they'd start up again. I often wound up saying, "If you'd just do it this way, then everything would be ok."

When you are surrounded by the disease of addiction, you live in chaos. Family members tend to control everything—to be controlling—in order to feel a sense of normalcy. As a result, family members become just as sick as the addict. That's why addiction is a family disease. I'll say it again. The most undiagnosed part of addiction is the family.

It's absolutely no coincidence that I attracted an addict because I grew up around many. After all, we attract who we are. I feel so grateful that I attracted one in recovery. That, my friends, is a miracle in itself. Preston was kind and patient. He loved me for who I was, and he trusted that I would find my way.

Recognizing that my behaviors were sick, too, after thinking I was a "normie," he encouraged me to find my own outlet.

Over time, with the help of Preston and a 12-step program for friends and families affected by the disease, I realized that my self-righteousness was fear. Fear that the man I had fallen in love with didn't have the perfect story, didn't look and sound exactly the way I had pictured in my dreams. Fear of what other people would think of him and of me for choosing him. Fear of how to handle this recovery thing I knew nothing about, and that seemed so shunned by society.

I wanted to make his addiction nice and perfect.

Though I didn't know it at the time, finding my own recovery was one of the best decisions I have ever made because I started learning about myself.

My addiction to pleasing, performing, and perfecting was just as sick as the alcoholic reaching for the bottle. Worse, I didn't need a drink or drug in me to act crazily!

I wanted to be more open and free with myself and others, rather than judgmental and closed-off. On the outside, I seemed confident, ballsy, and fun. I was. On the inside, I felt like nothing was ever enough to make me happy. I also felt tight and scared.

Today, as a full-time life coach and dedicated 12-step member, personal development and a spiritual way of being are the cornerstones of who I am. I strongly believe the world would be a drastically different place, for the better, if everyone was in a 12-step program.

As of the writing of this book, my husband celebrates 21 years clean and sober. He is 42.

I celebrate 14 years of a daily commitment to emotional sobriety in Al-Anon. I am 39.

Today, my husband does not crave a drink or a drug and hasn't for many, many years. He does crave escape, freedom, and a feeling of no responsibility. This shows up in many obsessive and selfish behaviors like coffee, sugar, and wanting to be left alone, all of which left unchecked could be dangerous to his sobriety. That's why he continues to go to meetings.

I crave being understood, a form of people-pleasing, and recently it's getting me into trouble. Practice makes progress. I continually use the tools of the program to grow and to give myself grace when I stumble.

Recovery, and its principles, create a common language and foundation in our relationship. As does a commitment to couple's counseling, which we advocate for all the time.

Addicts are beautiful human beings who are struggling with a disease. They require our compassion, not our judgment. They're your neighbors, they're your coworkers, they have families. They aren't the can't-get-it-together, brown-paper-bag-drinking underlings I thought they were. It's hard to believe I ever thought that was the case. Thank God I have evolved.

Many recovering addicts I know are afraid to be open about their sobriety. They are scared of how it might damage their professional reputation, of how people might judge them.

I understand this hesitation, this shame, because we have a long way to go as a society to reduce the stigma of addiction. Check out Preston's podcast, *The High Cost of Anonymity*,[20] as a great resource about how breaking your anonymity can be the best thing you ever did, and so much more about addiction and mental health. His profound message is helping so many people.

My husband and I choose to be open about, and proud of, our respective programs. We believe that, in sharing our stories, we literally may save someone's life. We may be the only example of recovery that person or that family ever sees. The number of times our honesty has led to a stranger being able to reach out for help is countless.

Anonymity is a key component of the 12-step world. While we respect that tradition and would never tell anyone to break it, we have found that being open works for us.

Today, I am grateful for my fun, fearful, and charismatic addict. He has taught me so much, and I wouldn't be half the woman I am today without him. Other days, I want to stab him between the eyes, and that seems perfectly normal.

The disease of alcoholism and recovery have changed my life immeasurably and set a tone that I am proud of and excited to have our child

---

[20] Preston Moore, host, *The High Cost of Anonymity* (podcast), Accessed March 18, 2023, https://open.spotify.com/show/65h0V990cXBZZ9Op20hYjA.

understand.

If you or a loved one is struggling with addiction or its effects, there is help and hope.

Do I want to be right or happy? Do I want to be perfect or human?

Sometimes I still want to be right and perfect.

As we say in the program, "That's why I keep coming back."

Talking in I, Not You

Have you ever noticed that people, including you, tend to tell stories in the second person? You will now. People do it all the time, and it's my pet peeve. Imagine a friend telling you about how running has changed her life. It sounds a little something like this:

"When you hit the road, it helps you get out of your head and sort out your shit. It helps you realize you're being crazy again, that you're focusing on the wrong things, and that you need to do better. You focus on getting to the end of the run rather than enjoying how far you've come. Running is who you are, you know?"

Does this sound odd to you? It does to me. I promise you that so many people talk this way. Talking in the second person about a first-hand experience is unbelievably common and, in my opinion, disempowering. We unconsciously create distance between ourselves and reality to make life more palatable and easier to digest, as if we're not the protagonist. Not many people take 100 percent responsibility for their lives. After all, playing the victim is tranquilizing. That's why we all do it so much.

Second-person language is one way we play the victim, one way we stave off vulnerability. Ownership over our experiences requires accountability and a growth mindset. Imagine if your friend shared this story about running instead:

"When I hit the road to run, I get out of my head and sort out my shit. I realize that I'm being crazy again, that I'm focusing on the wrong things, and that I need to do better. I often focus on getting to the end of the run rather than enjoying how far I've come. Running has become a part of who I am."

How does version two hit you differently?

For me, it's so much more powerful and riveting. To engage with someone who owns their experience gives me permission to own mine. First-person storytelling is where it's at.

Next Steps

After my treatment for depression and suicidal thinking, I found a part-time job working the front desk at a chiropractor's office. It was clear that the coaching position I accepted would take a while to ramp up, and I wanted to have a little income and structure to fall back on. In the coaching industry, we talk in big numbers. While I was training, I was told not to charge less than $100 per session. Shortly after I ventured out on my own, I joined a mastermind where the six-figure earnings mark was coveted. Want me to come and speak at your organization? That will be thousands.

Getting paid $15 an hour to woman a front desk was exactly what I wanted. It was simple. I needed something simple. It brought me back to recognizing the value of a dollar and recentered me around my core values. Working for myself was an emotional kaleidoscope, and it didn't always look pretty. Working at the chiropractor's office was easy. Until it wasn't.

It was a growing business, and I started to treat it as if it were mine. In the hours I wasn't working, I worried about how to market it, what systems it needed, how to welcome guests, etc. My ongoing therapy sessions were often consumed with my frustrations, and it was clear that my behavior was unmanageable. I was trying to control outcomes. I was erring into perfectionism, worried about whether I was doing a good enough job.

I had to experience this crisis in thinking to realize that this was my old pattern. I was overburdening myself and putting way too much on my shoulders trying to figure things out that weren't mine to figure out. I wanted to focus on what was within my control and what was my business. Their chiropractic business was not my business!

I was focusing on things outside of myself when my only job was to focus on my healing. External versus internal. I realized that I wanted to be less stiff and that I didn't want to get stuck forcing things that don't feel right. I wanted to be an easy-breezy person who flows through life, accepting abundance as it comes rather than manufacturing problems. I loved being at the front desk and chatting with everyone. I expanded my connection skills, and I also got to practice humility. There were moments when I wanted to scream, "I'm so much more than a front desk girl!"—aren't we all?—and instead, I let it be rather than manage people's image of me.

Choosing that job was the right choice for me at the time. But, over time, it became clear that it was starting to cost me money, and that's when I knew it was time to leave. I am so grateful for that brief yet meaningful stint where I nursed myself forward to wholeness. I say forward because there's no going back. The past stays in the past.

Since starting my coaching business again, my journey has been very different. In many ways, it has become exactly what I wanted it to be. Nothing changed except for me. I learned how to surrender. I learned how to create space for things to happen. I learned to not spend money I don't have. I learned patience. I let go of some entitlement.

There was a time when I often tried to enact everything. That created forcing and frustration. I've since learned the art of marination. It's an absolute gift. I learned that success doesn't live outside of me. It lives right here where I am. I have to be in love with what's happening now, who I am now, in order for it to get better.

I'm so grateful I got to the point of having suicidal thoughts because, with stakes that high, I had to do things differently. The toll was unbearable. I didn't want to die nor did I want to live with that level of fear and unpredictability. My body and mind were literally screaming at me to change. I chose to. I wanted to because the alternative was unthinkable.

Secrets are the hallmark of an alcoholic home, and suicidal thoughts often feel to me like dirty secrets. Let's pretend we're great to the outside world. Meanwhile, on the inside, we're dying. That's my whole story in a nutshell. Secrets thrive in the dark, so having a safe space to put them into the light was a relief. I'm doing the same in my work. I'm providing a safe room where you can share yourself exactly as you are.

We're all searching for rooms where we feel like we belong: church rooms, yoga rooms, family rooms, business rooms, shopping rooms, therapy rooms. We're in the business of finding and providing rooms where we feel safe enough to let down our guards so the light can filter in.

Find your room. Find your people. Find your passions. Let your guard down. Be your beautiful, messy self. You're worthy of the light. And, above all, find the audacity to love who you are.

Wouldn't Change a Thing

One approach to life that works for me is trusting where I'm standing. This is the exact opposite of how I felt at the Oprah event. I couldn't get into the circle and dance and feel free because I didn't trust myself.

Now, I trust the spot I'm standing in. I could easily be standing in a different spot. There are many decisions along the way that could have led me down other paths. Yet, if I daydream about what could have been, I step out of reality and into fantasy. What could have been isn't real. If one thing changes, everything changes. I know for sure this is where I'm supposed to be because I'm here.

Do you trust where you're standing?

Here's my advice. Don't get stuck in the messy middle. Instead, give yourself the absolute pleasure of taking radical responsibility for the beginning of your story. If you want to be somewhere or someone different, you haven't taken accountability for what got you here, where you are now.

You have the opportunity to do the work of accepting your reality, especially the parts you don't love, so you can create your future. So you can live the unlived life within you. So you can write your own ending.

That's being full of yourself.

Afterword

I wholeheartedly believe that when I create something it's for me first—create being the operative word. I wrote this book for myself and to take on a goal I have had for more than two decades. I write to know myself better, to retrace my story, to learn, and to heal. You'll notice that helping you is secondary to helping me. I have asked myself many times, *Is this any good? Will anyone even care that I have written this book?* And then I get to remind myself that whether or not anyone likes it or cares is none of my business. My only business is to remember that I care and to keep writing.

This is a very different lens from the lessons I learned in the first part of building my business. In the end, The Extravaganza, for example, was more about looking good and proving myself. My focus was external. When I now say, "It's about me first," what I mean is that it's about my internal world and the ways in which the work will change me, fulfill me, and heal me.

I get sick of hearing coaches, healers, social workers, and therapists say, "I just want to help people." I'm not a coach primarily to help my clients. I'm a coach first and foremost because it's the work that is in alignment for me. It's in alignment because it's healing for me, and it's fun. Another way I might say this is that it's God's work, meaning that I express the best of myself through being a coach. Helping others is secondary.

If I approached my work solely to help people, over time, I would experience resentment and burnout. I also wouldn't be modeling the work—to be self-reflective, to ask the hard questions, to dedicate time to my healing and evolution, to set boundaries, to understand myself.

These are the behaviors I look for in a coach I want to hire. I'm much more interested in who I observe someone to be than what they can do and their credentials. In other words, do I want what they have?

I brag that I want what I have in having committed to this book. The journey I have taken in bringing this book to life is the prize. I have pieced together stories and made sense of them. I have found compassion in places where there was none. I've connected with people from my past and healed wounds. I've come to understand myself in new ways and therefore created a new future. I've shown myself that I can set a goal and achieve it.

The wonderful by-product of my commitment is that I get to share it with you, and it might impact your life in some way. What happens when my book goes to market is the cherry on top. I'm the sundae, you're the cherry. In your own life, you're the sundae, and everyone else is the cherry. Too many people put too much focus on the feedback from the cherry.

Remember, there's a lot more sundae than there is cherry, and that's the right ratio of focus when it comes to valuing whose opinions and ideas matter most. I'm constantly moving in the direction of making my wants and needs a sundae-sized amount, and that keeps me full of myself. I hope the same for you. #bethesundae

Acknowledgments

I would like to acknowledge the heart and talent and wisdom and willingness of the following people.

To myself for having the courage to keep writing, especially when I didn't know what I was writing and if it was any good. For the persistence to bring it to completion.

To my parents, Charlie and Jennie, who provided me with a very unique and loving upbringing that paved the way for so much of who I am. I love you so, so, so, so much. I am incredibly lucky to have you.

To Heather Parady for saying to me, "You could just start writing," when I said that I wanted to write a book but needed to take some writing courses first. Thank God I listened to you and started writing. You and your words were in the very right place at the very right time.

To Clare Fernández, my wonderful, superbly talented editor. You had me at, "What makes me a great editor is that I read a lot of books." Working alongside you and being guided by you has been an absolute blessing. I have delighted in the thousands of little messages back and forth, your attention to detail, how you've cheerleaded me, and who you are. Here's to the beginning of a lifelong relationship and more lovely projects to come. These words have become a book that is immeasurably better thanks to you.

To my advanced readers, Preston Moore, Jennie Tonner, Emily Cockley, Joanne Ozug, and Cara Hollenbeck. Your feedback helped to shape this book and make it better. What you did, more importantly, was help me believe that this book could serve others. Thank you for your generous gifts of time and love.

To the coaching industry for existing, welcoming me into the fold, and nurturing me. I'm an Enneagram 3 so I like to be mindful that I am not what I do. And, I don't know who I'd be if coaching wasn't a part of my life. Special thanks to BetterUp who has matched me with clients I could only dream about and raised my confidence and abilities as a coach. I am so very grateful for your care and investment in me.

To all my wonderful clients who have shaped me and made me take a long hard look at myself. Yes, I was coaching you. And because of your vulnerability and willingness to do your work, I have been able to do more of my own. I can't believe we get to hang out and talk about cool shit like who you are, what you're struggling with, and who you'd like to become. More of that, please.

To the ladies in the Full of Herself Community. We have tested something over the last 18 months that I have loved. You have been by my side, loyal, and engaged. Thank you so much. Special, special thanks to you early adopters: Sarah Boreen, Veronica Rohach, Ellie Moore, Vanina Geranova, Alissa Mann, Melanie McCurry, Camille De Leonardis, and Emily Cockley.

To my Moore Soul Sessions Team, Veronica Rohach, Sharon Fancher, and Christina Easton. I pinch myself every day that I get to work with you all, and I feel so fancy saying "my team." You are examples of doing the work and your belief in what we do is the best gift this girl could ask for.

To Veronica, your consistent belief that what I do matters and knowing that it makes a difference in your life has kept me going on some hard days. The way you live inspires me and your straightforward communication is a big blessing.

To Sharon, your willingness to get outside of your comfort zone makes me fist bump with gratitude. Your optimism and zest for what we can create are everything I want. You make this business and me better.

To Christina, you came along and drastically improved our systems and processes in ways that delight me. You have elevated us all. Your attention to detail and love for radical communication makes me feel safe and supported, and I'm grateful we found each other.

To Mary McKinney, thank you for being with me almost from the beginning of the Moore Soul Sessions revival a few years back. Your willingness to work alongside me stoked my belief that this could be a real business and make a difference in women's lives. I treasure so deeply having had you to bounce my ideas off of. It made them seem real. You are a very talented young woman and I'm grateful to know you and watch you evolve.

To Shanda Trofe, your sweet and knowledgeable soul has taken a Google doc and made it into an actual book. *Say what!!* You have been the perfect partner to bring my story to life. I love your love of systems.

To Mary Rembert, thank you for your proofreader's eye.

To my previous Al-Anon sponsors, my current sponsor, and my friends in the program. You continue to save my life. What a principled life we get to live because of this fellowship.

To Austi, my sweet boy. You continue to reflect the work I need to do on myself that, most days, I'm willing enough to keep doing. I love you, and you'll always be my little munchie-boys. The process of writing this book is so much more important to who you'll become than to how it performs in the world.

To my husband, Preston. I want everyone to know that you were the first person to finish reading the advance copy of this book. You read it 2.5 times! This is one tiny example of how you love me so deeply and care about me in a million ways. I'm thankful I didn't leave Barnes & Noble and peace out to that party in Houston.

About the Author

Sarah T. Moore is a Women's Leadership Coach. With over a decade of experience, she coaches women to know what they want and to have the courage to speak it and pursue it. Whether she's a senior executive leading a global brand, a wife and mum who is tired of wondering if she's enough, or an entrepreneur trying to figure it all out … Sarah coaches clients who struggle with self-doubt and want more of one thing: wholeness.

Sarah is the creator of the Pump Up Session, a one-of-a-kind fully curated mini-retreat designed to help women reset their thoughts and quiet their internal chatter. She lives in Columbus, Ohio, with her husband, Preston, and their son, Austin.

Mooresoulsessions.com

 @moore.soul.sessions

My Coaching Philosophy

I believe every woman is special, and, oftentimes, our struggles aren't unique. My job, as your coach, is to help you become a more effective leader in every aspect of your life. I want to help you solve immediate problems that illuminate greater areas of development. That way you can self-coach your way to success long after our time together is over. Every question I ask, every moment I'm listening, and every request I have of you is to help you become more than you are right now, not to make you something you're not. You are the expert on you, and I'm the expert in coaching techniques.

The work starts with me being a leader in my own life, which means I take radical responsibility and practice honesty in a way most people don't. I also take a holistic approach to leadership because everything in our life affects our leadership at work. To compartmentalize is an outdated model. There are many techniques to become more effective, and it's my goal to help you discover what works for you. Nothing beats being guided by a coach who has incredible intuition, experience coaching thousands of women, and a deep desire to support the change you wish to see in yourself.

Want to Become More Full of Yourself?

If you enjoyed this book, now is the time to start applying the tools in your day-to-day life.

I have created a custom workbook that will help you personalize these skills, including a four-step **What do I think?** process that will change your life.

Self-doubt and worrying about what other people think of you doesn't have to be your story.

Download this workbook and continue your journey. We also included *bonus* stories that didn't make it into the book.

With love,

Sarah
x

www.ingramcontent.com/pod-product-compliance
Lightning Source LLC
Chambersburg PA
CBHW071140130626
46553CB00004B/1451